"A useful step by step guide for all those who wish to manage climate change in their organization. Brings the daunting macro challenge down to helpful concrete steps."

Christiana Figueres, Former Executive Secretary of the United Nations Framework Convention on Climate Change, and Founding Partner of www.GlobalOptimism.com

"Climate change is the ultimate systems thinking challenge. We should be thinking about how climate change is going to affect our communities, businesses, operations and missions. It's high time we had a "how to" guide for putting a strategic thinking hat on and tackling the unprecedented transformation we must undertake to ensure health, security and economic vitality in a changing world."

Daniel Kreeger, Executive Director, Association of Climate Change Officers

"The need for scenario planning has never been greater. The January 2019 PG&E bankruptcy was described by *The Wall Street Journal* as "*the first major corporate casualty of climate change.*" The same week, David Crane, former utility CEO, said that within two decades Amazon or Google will dominate electricity provision in the U.S. Haigh provides a valuable resource for climate strategists."

Gib Hedstrom, Author, "Sustainability: What It Is and How to Measure It"

"Climate related risks and transitions involve large uncertainties and long timeframes that are not often addressed with conventional strategic planning. The book offers a comprehensive, step-by-step process with helpful lists and tables to plan for an uncertain future. Leading an organization through the scenario planning process will not only result in a sound plan, but will increase management's understanding of the best ways to respond to potential impacts of climate change."

David Clark, Vice President, Sustainability, Amcor

SCENARIO PLANNING FOR CLIMATE CHANGE

Climate change, and the resultant impact on resource management and societal well-being, is one of the greatest challenges facing businesses and their long-term performance. Uncertainty about access to resources, unanticipated weather events, rapidly changing market conditions and potential social unrest is felt across all business and industry sectors. This book sets out an engaging step-by-step scenario planning method that executives, Board members, managers, and consultants can follow to develop a long-term strategy for climate change tailored for their business.

Most climate change strategy books discuss climate *mitigation*, focusing on how companies engage with carbon policy, new technologies, markets, and other stakeholders about reducing carbon emissions. This book explores these themes but also looks at strategizing for climate change *adaptation*. Adaptation is equally important, especially given that companies cannot negotiate with nature. There is a need to interpret climate science for business in a way that acknowledges the realities of climate change and identifies a way forwards in responding to this uncertain future.

Nardia Haigh is a business strategist for sustainability issues. Her research focuses on strategies and business models that address issues like climate change, the management of environmental commons, and pressing social issues. Nardia has researched these issues and consulted with companies about them, and her work appears in outlets including the *California Management Review, Journal of Business Ethics, European Management Journal, Organization & Environment*, and *Business Strategy and the Environment*. Dr Haigh has been cited in media outlets such as the *Guardian*, Ideas for Leaders, and Management INK. Nardia completed her Ph.D. in business management focusing on business strategies in response to climate change at the University of Queensland Business School, in Brisbane, Australia, and is as a tenured Associate Professor of Management at the University of Massachusetts Boston.

SCENARIO PLANNING FOR CLIMATE CHANGE

A Guide for Strategists

Nardia Haigh

Routledge
Taylor & Francis Group

LONDON AND NEW YORK

First published 2019
by Routledge
2 Park Square, Milton Park, Abingdon, Oxon OX14 4RN

and by Routledge
711 Third Avenue, New York, NY 10017

Routledge is an imprint of the Taylor & Francis Group, an informa business

© 2019 Nardia Haigh

British Library Cataloguing-in-Publication Data
A catalogue record for this book is available from the British Library

Library of Congress Cataloging-in-Publication Data
Names: Haigh, Nardia, author.
Title: Scenario planning for climate change : a guide for strategists / Nardia Haigh.
Description: First Edition. | New York : Routledge, 2019.
Identifiers: LCCN 2018056681| ISBN 9781138498389 (hardback) | ISBN 9781138498402 (pbk.) | ISBN 9781351016353 (ebook)
Subjects: LCSH: Climatic changes--Government policy.
Classification: LCC QC902.9 .H35 2019 | DDC 363.738/7456--dc23
LC record available at https://lccn.loc.gov/2018056681

ISBN: 978-1-138-49838-9 (hbk)
ISBN: 978-1-138-49840-2 (pbk)
ISBN: 978-1-351-01635-3 (ebk)

Typeset in Bembo
by Taylor & Francis Books

CONTENTS

ILLUSTRATIONS

Figures

Tables

Boxes

ACKNOWLEDGMENTS

In writing a book that I hope brings knowledge and a useful method to others who are strategizing for climate change, I need to acknowledge the support and work of many people. My most important supporter was my partner in life, Ed Carberry, who never failed to be there throughout the entire process, and who gave me a copy of *Thinking Like Your Editor* by Rabiner & Fortunato, which helped me start the book after years of honing the method. Andrew Hoffman has been a great mentor (and on other projects a great co-author), to whom I am grateful for advice on book writing, feedback on the proposal, referrals to publishers (including Routledge!), and the push to "write the book you want to write." Another great mentor and co-author is Andrew Griffiths, who introduced me to scenario planning back in 2002 when I was doing my Masters, and changed the way I think. In 2005, Andrew took me on as a Ph.D. student studying organizational response to climate change, and during that time involved me as a teaching assistant in executive education at the intersection of scenario planning and climate change. This all created the intersection of topics you see in this book. Gail Whiteman, Brian Halley, Martina Linnenluecke, Laura Devenney and Mark Trexler reviewed the book proposal and provided valuable critique. Paul Kirshen, Bob Massie and Andrew Griffiths also read and critiqued the proposal, and also wrote wonderful letters of support to accompany it. Thank you! Sara Murphy, Greg Porter, Kate Dougherty, Matt Urdan, and Chinmai Hemani provided research assistance that helped me complete the climate driver summaries in the appendix, and others that are freely available at www.nardiahaigh.com. Finally, the book would not have been possible without the almost 450 executives and students to whom I have taught scenario planning, and with whom I have discussed and sometimes debated climate change, scenario planning, and the intersection of the two. Without you, I would not have had the opportunity to develop the method to a point at which it could be codified. Thank you.

A NOTE TO THE READER

In this book I offer a framework to help find a solution to a problem. The problem is climate change, which already poses a significant and complex range of short-term and long-term issues to many organizations, and will do so far into the future. Scenario planning, which offers a powerful approach to long-term and short-term strategic management, can help you find your solution to climate change.

The main audience for this book is decision-makers who want to develop a climate change strategy for their organization. The body of the book provides the method, and at the back of the book is an appendix containing summaries of commonly identified climate change trends. Other summaries of climate trends are available for free download at www.nardiahaigh.com. Together, the method and the summaries will give you the basics of what you need to begin a climate change scenario planning project to develop your climate change strategy.

The method outlined in the book stands on the shoulders of others who are cited in the introduction. Previous work on the topic of scenario planning has often focused on large, well-known companies and consulting houses that have a wealth of in-house knowledge about and experience with scenario planning. Similarly, much climate change research, including some of my own, has been conducted using samples of large companies. One goal I have in writing this book is to make insights about scenario planning and strategizing for climate change more accessible to all organizations. To that end, this book provides a practical step-by-step method that a manager in any organization could use to put together a scenario planning project to develop a climate change strategy.

In an age of surprising and devastating climatic trends and events, the need for scenario planning to develop climate change strategies has never been greater.

INTRODUCTION

Having opened this book, you likely understand that regardless of your ideological leanings on climate change, or the state of policy in any given country at any specific point in time, it is increasingly important to understand how climate change will shape the future of business.

It is a rare day that something related to climate change is not covered by news media. A simple search using Google shows that in the two years to 30 June 2018, there were on average more than 250,000 news stories per month using the term "climate change," and over the past decade, the number of news stories using the term has grown from approximately 19,200 to 1,630,000 per year.[1] Many recent news stories relay the latest climate science discoveries, while others are thick with rhetoric and opinion. They run the gamut of topics from physical issues like rising sea levels and rising temperatures, to technological innovations aimed at curbing or sequestering carbon emissions, and debates surrounding international climate policy and the Paris Climate Agreement. These media can give some insight into how climate change is broadly affecting your country, region, and occasionally your industry, but they cannot answer the question "How could climate change affect my organization?" and therefore cannot answer the equally important question of "What should we be doing about it?" This book will teach you a method to find and interpret climate science, anecdotal stories, and other evidence to answer these questions, so your organization can develop a rigorous but flexible long-term climate change strategy.

Climate change affects organizations

Climate change refers to long-term changes in the broader climate (not shorter-term weather), and accommodates anthropogenic (human-caused) changes, as well as changes that are naturally occurring. Below is the International Panel on Climate Change's (IPCC's) definition of climate change:

> *Climate change refers to a change in the state of the climate ... that persists for an extended period, typically decades or longer. Climate change may be due to natural internal processes or external forcings such as modulations of the solar cycles, volcanic eruptions and persistent anthropogenic changes in the composition of the atmosphere or in land use.*[1]

Climate change can affect your organization in many ways, but three types of impacts stand out – changes in the physical natural environment, changes in policy, and changes in shareholder and/or market sentiment.

The first and most fundamental impact is through climate change in the physical natural environment, which can affect assets and infrastructure, suppliers, and markets. Regardless of which side you occupy in debates about the impact of industrial activity on climate change, the fact remains that organizations cannot negotiate with nature, and yet they exist within its physical confines. Regardless of which industry your organization is in, all the resources it needs, like energy, minerals, food, water, building materials, land, and air are ultimately derived from a natural environment with which you cannot negotiate. Consider the following examples.

Organizations that found ways to adapt to physical climate change have been farmers in the Okanagan Valley in British Columbia, Canada, who noticed their warming winters early. Douglas Belkin reported in the *Wall Street Journal*[2] that the Okanagan Valley region has historically been dairy farming and apple growing country, but since 1947 the growing season has increased by 11 days and the average summer temperature has become 4°F warmer. Farmers began capitalizing on the increasing temperature by planting a more profitable crop – grapes – and early movers have benefited greatly, because their vines are now maturing and producing quality wine. These farmers already had deep connections with the land through their other agricultural practices, and developed a strategy to make the new emerging physical environment work for them. They were able to leverage their existing agricultural capabilities and knowledge of their land, while developing new skills for the new crop. As a result, between 1987 and 2007 the value of land in Okanagan Valley increased from US$5,000 to US$200,000 an acre (a massive increase in the value of a key asset), and from 1990 to 2007 the number of wineries in British Columbia increased from 17 to 136. A variation on the Okanagan Valley winemakers' story is being echoed all around the world, as winemakers from Australia to France seek out cooler locations to retain the ability to produce high quality wine.[3]

Other businesses have struggled with the impacts. The 2011–2017 California drought had a significant and detrimental effect on the State's almond crops. Blue Diamond Growers, a cooperative owned by half of California's almond growers, is one organization that has felt the effects of the drought. In a 2014 monthly market update, Blue Diamond Growers reported that the year's crop would be smaller than projected (read, produce less revenue) due to an early harvest and smaller crop associated with "rain-free weather" and that 2015 would be similar.[4] The lack of rain prompted Blue Diamond's network of almond growers to collectively invest

US$3 Billion in "smart irrigation systems" to reduce their consumption of water.[5] By late 2016 the outlook was better, ample rain and snow produced a healthier crop, and 75% of California had been declared drought-free by the U.S. Drought Monitor.[6] However, by mid–March 2017 the tables had turned and high rainfall threatened to damage almond blooms and disrupt bees' willingness to fly and pollinate them.[7] Further, while rain broke the *surface water* drought, *groundwater* has not recovered and may not for years.[8] Adding to this, policymakers had altered irrigation allocations in some regions because of the drought, and they have not been reset, so farmers did not receive a full water allocation in 2017.[9] A combination of low rainfall and high surface temperatures made this an archetype climate change drought that also brought more of California's familiar wildfires and some of the lowest water storage and snowpack levels on record.[10] Blue Diamond's experience is an example of what can occur as global temperatures rise, precipitation patterns change, and more precipitation falls as rain rather than snow. Droughts like it were projected by the IPCC's 2014 regional report.[11]

If the above examples about wine and almonds lead you to assume only agricultural organizations might be affected, then consider that any organization operating in or serving Shishmaref, Alaska, is facing great disruption and costs as the entire village of approximately 600 people moves to avoid coastal erosion caused by melting sea ice and storm surges. Christopher Mele and Daniel Victor reported in *The New York Times*[12] that since 1969, Shishmaref (which is on Sarichef Island) has lost more than 200 feet of its shoreline to erosion, including the loss of infrastructure and buildings. Online searches of Google Maps and chamberofcommerce. com show a long and varied list of affected organizations, including the airport, United States Postal Service, State Police, the electricity company, a civil engineering and construction company, an electrician and general contractor, a University of Alaska Anchorage campus, Shishmaref School, Shishmaref Native Store, Nayok General Store, a tannery, a laundromat, a community center, Shismaref Lutheran Church, a barge serving the island, Norton Sound Health Corporation, water and telecommunications utilities, and the City of Nome (since Shishmaref is within Nome's census area). The cost of moving the village is estimated to be US $180 Million according to Mele and Victor, and even though the plan is to move just five miles to mainland Alaska, the disruption to people and organizations will be significant, and some organizations may be left with stranded assets, or become obsolete if others like them are already established in the new location.

A second way that climate change can affect your organization is through the development of city, state, and national policies to regulate, reduce, and put a price on carbon emissions, driven primarily by ratification of the Kyoto Protocol. The Kyoto Protocol is an international treaty of the United Nations Framework Convention on Climate Change (UNFCCC), which was ratified in 2005 and obligated developed nations to reduce their carbon emissions on the basis that climate change is occurring and that man's industrial activity is contributing to it.[13] Since 2005, there have been many meetings working on its implementation, with the most recent Paris Climate Accord agreeing the details of how international mitigation and adaptation efforts will be financed, undertaken, and reported, and how each country will contribute to those efforts.

As countries negotiate their roles and obligations under the international agreement, and even decide whether they want in or out of it, businesses within each country consider the possible implications for themselves. Much research by myself and others[14, 15, 16, 17] has found that at the first inkling of potential policy, businesses in carbon-intensive sectors like electricity, oil and gas, and mining, typically lobby to prevent, stall, or water down carbon regulation arguing that it will increase costs, increase the price of their products and potentially create stranded assets by reducing the viability of existing long-term investments. On the other hand, companies that are less carbon-intensive, such as renewable energy companies and manufacturers of energy efficient products, will simultaneously lobby to accelerate, broaden, and strengthen policy to regulate and put a price on carbon emissions; arguing that their products and technologies are needed to meet international obligations. This tug-of-war can sway governments one way or the other in response to corporate, NGO, constituent, and international pressure, and in turn bring a great deal of uncertainty to businesses needing to make long-term investments in capital assets, products, and markets. Policies to reduce carbon emissions can translate into such things as rebates for investing in renewable technologies (e.g. cogeneration or solar power), the opportunity to invest in new carbon markets (e.g. the EU Emissions Trading System), more choice among energy efficient technologies (e.g. electric vehicles), but also potentially increase taxes (e.g. a carbon tax) or the price of fossil fuels at the gas pump or electricity meter depending on the policy measure implemented.

A third way that climate change can affect businesses is through changes in market and shareholder sentiment. In particular, shareholders are becoming activists, and are using shareholder resolutions, which are voted on by all shareholders at annual general meetings, to compel companies to act on climate change through such things as altering their investments in fossil fuels, and reporting their potential climate change vulnerabilities. Exxon has been a target of shareholder activists for some time, and in 2017 the new CEO Darren Woods faced resolutions demanding that Exxon cut new oil field investments and instead give shareholders a larger dividend, and demanding the company use climate change accounting methods to quantify its climate change risk.[18] These types of resolutions are gaining traction with Exxon's shareholders as activists increasingly frame them in terms of broad shareholder interests. In a survey by law firm Schulte Roth & Zabel,[19] corporations expected shareholder activism to grow in coming years, and this is supported by the growth of organizations such as Ceres (a non-profit that advocates for sustainability leadership) that has been instrumental in advocating for action on climate change through its networks. Your organization may not be in a carbon-intensive industry as is Exxon, and it may not be a multi-national corporation, but as shareholder awareness of climate change and its potential to affect investments like retirement nest eggs grows, it is increasingly likely that shareholders of both private and publicly listed companies will voice their concerns about how their investments could be affected by climate change over the long term.

Climate change brings uncertainty

A characteristic shared by many of the climate change issues described above is that they can bring uncertainty to organizational strategizing, because they are dynamic and largely beyond the control of decision-makers. Research conducted by Katy Maher and Janet Peace at the Center for Climate and Energy Solutions[20] suggests that you may already be feeling some of this uncertainty. They found that businesses are increasingly concerned about climate change risks to public infrastructure providing electricity, water, communications, roads, and public transport, which in turn affect operations (but are all outside the control of a single organization). Maher and Peace's research shows that businesses are also concerned about how exposed their suppliers are to the same issues. As one of their research subjects stated, "you are only as resilient as your weakest link, so it is important to identify where that link is."

Uncertainties can make strategizing complex, but as eminent scenario planner Peter Schwartz said, "The world may be uncertain and unpredictable but that's no excuse for being unprepared."[21] The scenario planning method laid out in this book will help you manage a considerable amount of uncertainty without over-simplifying it. There is much information available on climate change, its impacts, and mitigation and adaptation strategies that just need to be interpreted for organizations, including your organization, so you can identify and address your own "weakest links." In the back of the book, the Appendix provides overview summaries for a sample of known driving forces of climate change, to help you determine how they may already be affecting your organization, or may affect it in future.

Organizational responses to climate change

In response to the climate change issues mentioned above, and others, your organization has several broad options for action. Where other people are involved – shareholders, policymakers, customers, suppliers, etc. – you may be able to communicate, negotiate, or lobby for more favorable conditions. For instance, you can negotiate with shareholder activists to withdraw or amend a shareholder resolution, and if your organization, industry association, or chamber of commerce is powerful enough, you may be able to sway policymakers. You can also communicate with customers and suppliers to understand their needs (and relay your own). However, your options when responding to changes in physical natural environment are limited to: (a) Adapting strategies, operations, assets and/or infrastructure to become resilient to unfavorable conditions (or to leverage conditions changing in your favor). This includes making changes to your physical environment; (b) Avoiding unfavorable conditions, or pursuing more favorable conditions, by relocating; or (c) Doing neither and experiencing the full force of whatever conditions unfold, and adapting on the fly where possible.

To respond with the greatest likelihood of success, this book will teach you a method of scenario planning to find what is driving physical, policy, shareholder, and other changes that could affect your organization. It will teach you how to develop a range of potential scenarios based on the drivers you identify, and how to translate those scenarios into a climate change strategy you can use to move forward with increased confidence.

What is scenario planning?

Scenario planning is the development of multiple scenarios about the future, and use of them to make decisions. In his organizational adaptation book, William Fulmer emphasized the need for organizations to consider "what if" questions about the future, so decision-makers are prompted to think ahead.[22] Scenarios are plausible hypothetical "what if" stories about what your organization's future might look like based on forces that could shape it. Scenarios are not projections, predictions, or forecasts, but are powerful narratives to help you anticipate and prepare for possible changes your organization might encounter in future. As Hawken, Ogilvy, and Schwartz noted in their early scenario book, *Seven Tomorrows*, the aim of scenarios is to "project alternative futures so that responsible and intelligent choice is possible."[23]

The aim of scenario planning is not to predict the future (as a forecast or projection might attempt). Rather, scenario planning recognizes that we live in an uncertain world and are limited in our ability to control or predict the future, and works with that uncertainty by considering how issues might develop along different pathways.[24] Scenario planning "allows for the inclusion of realism and imagination, comprehensiveness and uncertainty, and most of all ... plurality of options."[23]

Former Royal Dutch Shell scenario planner Pierre Wack noted that scenario planning can serve you in two main ways: (a) by helping you anticipate and understand your risk exposure; and (b) by helping you identify strategic options of which you are currently unaware.[25] The broad set of potential futures to which decision-makers are exposed are complete with both challenges and opportunities, to help people: Perceive change emerging over the horizon; identify early warning signals; prepare for potential surprises; identify effective ways to respond; and communicate it all with important stakeholders.[26, 27, 28] Scenario planning is useful for businesses that face high uncertainty, have experienced costly surprises, find it difficult to generate opportunities, are bureaucratic, are in a changing industry, or whose competitors are using scenario planning.[28]

Scenario planning links your organization to the future by making you think about what would be required in a range of possible futures, and compare those requirements to current resources, capabilities, operations, policies, strategies, and administrative practices. Scenario planning also links the future to the present by enabling you to situate shorter-term strategies within the longer-term scenarios to see how they may play out. If your organization has a strategic plan in place, then it is already considering and preparing for one scenario. How much more resilient could your organization become if it prepared for other possible scenarios? It would likely become significantly more resilient.

A little scenario planning history

The purpose of this book is not to recall the complete history of scenario planning. The likes of Malaska and Virtanen,[29] van der Heijden,[30] Lindgren and Bandhold,[31] Chermack,[32] Schwartz,[24] and Martelli[33] all provide good overviews for those wanting to read about the history of scenario planning; however, it is useful to know a little about where scenario planning started.

The use of scenario planning dates back to the 16th century, when Luis de Molina and his contemporaries considered that the future may not be a pre-determined singular path, but rather a set of "futuribles" or what Pentti Malaska and Ilkka Vertanen called a "fan of possible futures."[29] Fast-forward to the 1950s, Herman Kahn used it to help the U.S. military forecast and strategize,[31] and in France, futurist Gaston Berger and colleagues were also using scenario planning.[26] During the 1960s and 1970s, a dedicated group of people at Royal Dutch Shell developed and experimented with scenario planning in detail,[30, 34] which famously led the company to anticipate and prepare for potential opportunities and threats, including the 1970s oil crisis and the 1980s Iran–Iraq conflict.[26, 30, 34]

In the 1990s, Shell's scenario planning efforts recognized that climate change threats were emerging, and this led to climate change being acknowledged in its 1998 sustainability report (one of the first sustainability reports to acknowledge climate change).[26] In 2003, Peter Schwartz and Doug Randall[35] used scenario planning at the national level to assess the potential consequences of climate change for U.S. national security, food, water, and energy. At the global level, the IPCC[1, 36] also uses scenarios to determine possible futures based on differing levels of atmospheric carbon.

Many companies have followed the lead of early scenario planners, and today it is an integral element of many companies' strategy-making processes.[30] A global survey of over 8,500 executives regularly conducted by Bain & Company showed that the use of scenario and contingency planning nearly doubled after the 9/11 terrorist attacks. After its 2006 survey, Darrell Rigby and Barbara Bilodeau of Bain & Company reported that 65% of companies studied were expecting to use scenario and contingency planning in the near future (up from 38% in 1993). Rigby and Bilodeau believe their results show that businesses recognize an "increasing need to anticipate crises and develop robust contingency plans."[37]

The need to apply scenario planning to climate change

Scenario planning is eerily and perfectly suited to climate change, because many climate change trends are long-term and systemic, and because climate science projects the state of many physical impacts long into the future. In its 2002 report, *Abrupt Climate Change*, the National Research Council[38] recommended generating scenarios to understand potential abrupt climate change, and scenario planners such as Angela Wilkinson,[39] James Ogilvy,[23] Paul Hawken,[23] Peter Schwartz,[23, 40] and

Rafael Ramírez[39] have all specifically noted the usefulness of scenario planning for climate change. The Intergovernmental Panel on Climate Change has been developing global climate change scenarios for many years.[1]

The usefulness of strategizing for climate change is also now understood on Wall Street, especially since in 2010 the U.S. Securities Exchange Commission published guidelines to help companies disclose material climate change risks, and Ceres created an online Sustainability Disclosure Tool[41] that provides the public with easy access to climate change risks that companies have disclosed. To assist climate change risk disclosure efforts, the Financial Stability Board Task Force on Climate-Related Financial Disclosures (TCFD) recently advised companies to use scenario planning to analyze and understand the risks and opportunities that climate change may bring,[42] and described scenario planning as:

> ... an important and useful tool for an organization to use, both for understanding strategic implications of climate-related risks and opportunities and for informing stakeholders about how the organization is positioning itself in light of these risks and opportunities.

In their book *Predictable Surprises*, Harvard Professor of Business Administration, Max Bazerman, and his colleague Michael Watkins advocated the use of scenario planning to identify potential "predictable surprises."[43] They anticipated that climate change would become a predictable surprise, or "event[s] ... that take an individual or group by surprise, despite prior awareness of all of the information necessary to anticipate the events and their consequences." They argued that businesses would only avoid climate change surprises if they establish systems to recognize, prioritize, and mobilize for them. In previous research, I found that among a sample of businesses across various industries, only 61% had recognized climate change issues, 43% had progressed to prioritizing them, and only 22% had gone further to mobilize to do anything about them.[44] Other of my own research suggests that businesses struggle with climate change issues – in one study of organizational response to climate change issues, organizations I studied only responded to climate change issues on the fly after they had been surprised by their physical impacts.[45] Bazerman and Watkins' work and my own research both suggest that unless you invest time and energy to understand how climate change may affect your organization, it will likely be surprised.

The aim of this book is to improve your recognition and prioritization of, and mobilization in response to climate change issues so that your organization is prepared. Decision-makers who can anticipate a broader array of potential future states have greater capabilities to defend against threats and leverage opportunities, and can address some of the limitations of traditional strategy development approaches, such as its short time horizons and focus on a single desired future, which are discussed in detail in Chapter 1.

Having had an introduction to how climate change can affect businesses and to scenario planning, below is an overview of the method.

The scenario planning method

The scenario planning method in this book has four main steps, illustrated in Figure 0.1. Each step contains sub-steps, and covers a mixture of scenario planning content and project logistics. The steps are described briefly below, and are covered in great detail in Chapter 2 through Chapter 5. Links to online education modules based on the method are also accessible via www.nardiahaigh.com.

This method stands on the shoulders of those who have gone before, and recognizes there is no best method to undertake scenario planning, no best number of steps, and no best way to determine a successful scenario planning effort. It is a method that has benefited from the published scenario planning expertise of Peter Schwartz,[24] Pierre Wack,[25, 34] Shell,[27] Rafael Ramírez and Angela Wilkinson,[39] Thomas Chermack,[32] Bill Ralston and Ian Wilson,[46] Mats Lindgren and Hans Bandhold,[31] the TCFD,[42] and others, and is applied specifically to climate change. It is also the culmination of my own experience applying and refining the method, and teaching it to over 450 executives and students over more than a decade. It is a rich and analytical method that complements the qualitative knowledge, skills, and professional intuition of you, your colleagues, and other key stakeholders, with your needs to quantify some aspects of the project.

Like all scenario planning methods, it will challenge you, and later chapters will explain those challenges and how to manage them. Like all scenario planning methods, it can also be iterative (as indicated by the arrows in Figure 0.1). Many scenario planning books overlook the iteration involved with scenario planning, and I will explain where it can occur. If followed closely, the method will produce focused scenarios that will suggest what your organization can do now and in future to adapt to the positive and negative implications of climate change.

Step 1: Set the agenda, focal question and time horizon, and identify key stakeholders

As the heading suggests, Step 1 is a collection of four sub-steps to set the agenda, define the focal question and time horizon, and identify key stakeholders. It will cover the planning you need to undertake to get your scenario planning project off the ground, by helping you identify who could champion the project (ideally, the Chairman of the Board or CEO), who should lead the project and be on the team, and to determine a suitable duration and budget for the project. The overarching points here are to ensure the project is supported from the top with a champion and a budget, and that your team includes as many executives as is practical and is inclusive of all parts of the organization. With this planning done, you will learn how to define the focal question that scenario planning will answer for you. A sample question is suggested: "How could climate change plausibly affect our organization, what should we do, and when?" You can develop a different question if needed, perhaps one that is more specific surrounding one production plant, asset, or market, or a question that is more deductive in nature; focusing on

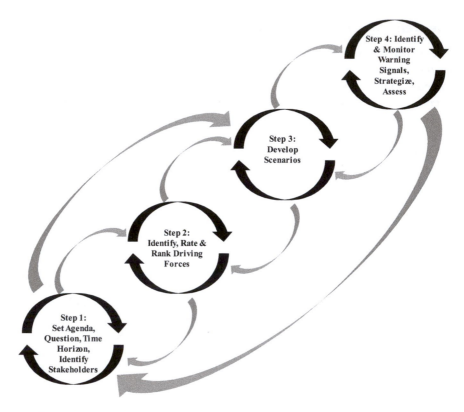

FIGURE 0.1 Scenario planning method

exploring different paths to one specific outcome, depending on your needs. You will also define a scenario planning time horizon that is appropriate for your organization. The book centers on a 25-year time horizon, but if this is not appropriate for your organization, you will be shown how to choose a more appropriate one. Finally, you will identify key stakeholders inside and outside the organization that are relevant to your focal question, such as key suppliers or partners that may be affected by climate change.

Step 2: Identify, rate and rank the driving forces

Step 2 is where the bulk of your analytical efforts will occur, since good scenarios depend on the ability of the project team to identify and analyze underlying driving forces that will shape the organization's future. Driving forces are such things as sea level change, drought, the implementation of policy, or changes in market sentiment relating to climate change, and potentially to the goods and services your organization provides. To get you started, the Appendix contains summaries for a sample of known climate change driving forces, including how they are affecting organizations now and how these impacts could play out in 25 years. More summaries are available at www.nardiahaigh.com, and these summaries are updated periodically. This step will guide you through the analytical process of identifying driving forces, rating the uncertainty of each, and rating the degree to which each could affect the organization if it were to occur. In addition to research, this analytical process will also draw on your expertise and that of your team, since you know your organization best. You will be guided through the rating process to ensure you are prepared to avoid potential stumbling blocks. The outcome of this step is a ranked list of climate change drivers that are, in combination, most uncertain and most impactful for your organization, and that could (because of the uncertainty) plausibly go in various directions in future. In Lindgren and Bandhold's words, you will have identified important "wild cards."[31]

Step 3: Develop the scenarios

Using your ranked list of climate change driving forces, the method will help you develop four plausible scenarios based on the two highest-ranking driving forces identified in Step 2, and show you how to incorporate some of the lower-ranking driving forces where appropriate. You will also undertake some quality control to ensure each scenario makes sense and is internally consistent, before you present a set of initial scenarios for feedback, and then use feedback to develop your final scenarios. The outcome of this step is a set of four detailed scenario narratives that describe how your organization could be affected by combinations of climate change drivers at the chosen time horizon, and explain how each scenario could have emerged from the present day. You will be given insights about how to present your scenarios to others, and suggestions about how to work through their feedback to build useful scenarios that will help you strategize.

Step 4: Identify warning signals, develop a climate change strategy, and assess the scenario planning process

The final step is a process of identifying warning signals, outlining a strategy that will prepare the organization for whatever scenario unfolds, and assessing your experiences with the process. Identifying warning signals is an important process of detecting what the organization should track so it can determine which scenario might be unfolding as time proceeds. Basic warning signals are those relating to each driver, such as the amount of sea level change or the implementation of climate policy initiatives at various levels of government, while others may be secondary or tertiary indicators that are not immediately apparent but are nonetheless important to track. The next sub-step is developing a climate change strategy that identifies actions the organization needs to take or could take regardless of which scenario unfolds, and actions it may need to take at certain points in future contingent upon warning signal indicators. As was the case with scenario development, this step includes developing a draft strategy for feedback, and then using the feedback to produce the outcome of the entire process: A rigorous but flexible long-term climate change strategy based on multiple plausible futures. This step also includes ways to complement scenario planning with existing strategic planning processes, and will prompt you to make a commitment to redoing your scenario planning process at regular intervals or when the situation changes. Finally, to provide a feedback loop that will build your in-house scenario planning skills and capabilities, the final sub-step is to assess your scenario planning project to understand its effectiveness, and to improve it for next time.

How to use this book

Scenario planning is a practice. It is participatory.[24] In my experience, Rafael Ramírez and Angela Wilkinson's statement below rings true:

> ... learning scenario planning is like riding a bicycle: you can read all the "how to" guide books and operating manuals, and someone can tell you how to ride it, but you only know how to ride after you get on the bike, feel the balance and turn the pedals, and even fall off a few times. So too with learning scenario planning; like learning to cycle, it requires practice and reflection as well as engaged fun.[39]

To that end, I would emphasize using this book to do, rather than just to think, about scenario planning for climate change.

The book is divided into seven chapters. The Introduction has introduced you to scenario planning and climate change and given you an overview of the method. Chapter 1 takes you through some of the limitations of current strategizing and the strengths of scenario planning, as well as some of the challenges involved in scenario planning. Chapter 2 through Chapter 5 set out the scenario planning method in detail, which you can follow (including hints and tips on process and logistics). The Conclusion wraps up what you will likely have achieved if you've followed the method, and offers concluding thoughts. Finally, to put you on a fast track, the Appendix in the back of the book provides summaries for a sample of climate change drivers to help you start thinking about how climate change might affect your organization now and 25 years into the future, and if you need more inspiration, any updated summaries and summaries for other drivers are available at www.nardiahaigh.com, along with links to online education modules based on the book.

In just a few hours, you can skim through the book quickly to grasp the overall method, and then dive more deeply into each step and make a start on your own scenario planning project. By doing this, my aim is to give you confidence that, in most cases, scenario planning skills can be developed in-house, or with facilitation and costs that run at the lower end of costs estimated by Harvard Business School[47] back in 2000, which ranged from around US$10,000–20,000 for smaller projects to well over US$1 Million for large projects. Even today, the upper ranges of this estimate can be prohibitive or simply not justifiable for businesses that are not multi-national corporations, and this book will enable you to run a substantial scenario planning project for far less.

Note

1   Figures derived using Google searches for news stories using the term "climate change" each month from June 30 2016 until June 30 2018, and each year from June 2008 to June 2018.

References

1   IPCC. 2014. *Climate Change 2014: Synthesis Report. Contribution of Working Groups I, II and III to the Fifth Assessment Report of the Intergovernmental Panel on Climate Change*, ed. R.K. Pachauri and L.A. Meyer, Geneva: IPCC.

2   Belkin, D. 2007. Northern vintage: Canada's wines rise with mercury, *The Wall Street Journal Online*, New York.

3   CBS. 2018. How wineries from Oregon to France are adapting to climate change, *CBS News*, 28 June 2018. https://www.cbsnews.com/news/wineries-adapting-climate-change/.

4   Blue Diamond Almonds. 2014. Blue Diamond Almonds – Industry Update – December 9, 2014. Blue Diamond Almonds. http://www.bdingredients.com/blue-diamond-almonds-industry-update-december-9-2014/, accessed 2 January 2015.

5   Page, S. 2016. Blue Diamond: Growing California's Almond Industry with Less Water. Harvard Business School. https://rctom.hbs.org/submission/blue-diamond-growing-californias-almond-industry-with-less-water/, accessed 2 July 2017.

6   U.S. Drought Monitor. 2017. *California*. http://droughtmonitor.unl.edu/Home/StateDroughtMonitor.aspx? CA, accessed 25 March 2017.

7   Post Online Media. 2017. Heavy rains hurt pollination and may hurt California almonds. *Post Online Media*. http://www.poandpo.com/agrifish/heavy-rains-hurt-pollination-and-may-hurt-california-almonds-2532017656/, accessed 25 March 2017.

8   Harter, T. 2017. Post-drought groundwater in California: Like the economy after a deep "recession," recovery will be slow. *PublicCEO*. http://www.publicceo.com/2017/03/post-drought-groundwater-in-california-like-the-economy-after-a-deep-recession-recovery-will-be-slow/, accessed 25 March 2017.

9   Associated Press. 2017. Agency: California farmers will get bump in irrigation water. *Daily Mail*. http://www.dailymail.co.uk/wires/ap/article-4340502/Agency-California-farmers-bump-irrigation-water.html, accessed 25 March 2017.

10 AghaKouchak, A., L. Cheng, O. Mazdiyasni and A. Farahmand. 2014. Global warming and changes in risk of concurrent climate extremes: Insights from the 2014 California drought, *Geophysical Research Letters*, 41/24: 8847–8852.

11 IPCC. 2014. *Climate Change 2014: Impacts, Adaptation, and Vulnerability. Part B: Regional Aspects. Contribution of Working Group II to the Fifth Assessment Report of the Intergovernmental Panel on Climate Change*, ed. V.R. Barros, et al. Cambridge & New York: Cambridge University Press.

12 Mele, C. and D. Victor. 2016. Reeling from effects of climate change, Alaskan village votes to relocate. *The New York Times*. https://www.nytimes.com/2016/08/20/us/shishmaref-alaska-elocate-vote-climate-change.html?_r=0, accessed 25 August 2016.

13 United Nations Framework Convention on Climate Change. UNFCCC website. http://unfccc.int/, accessed 21 July 2017.

14 Haigh, N. 2008. A view backstage of climate change environmental markets, *Australasian Journal of Environmental Management*, 15: 76–83.

15 Kolk, A. and J. Pinkse. 2007. Multinationals' political activities on climate change, *Business and Society*, 42/2: 201–228.

16 Ikwue, T. and J. Skea. 1994. Business and the genesis of the European Community carbon tax proposal, *Business Strategy and the Environment*, 3/2: 1–10.

17 Jones, C.A. and D.L. Levy. 2007. North American business strategies towards climate change, *European Management Journal*, 25/6: 428–440.

18 Carroll, J. 2017. Exxon, climate change activists to square off at shareholders meeting. *New Orleans Business News*. http://www.nola.com/business/index.ssf/2017/05/exxon_squares_off_with_shareho.html, accessed 22 July 2017.

19 Schulte Roth & Zabel. 2014. *Shareholder Activism Insight: A Schulte Roth & Zabel LLP report in association with mergermarket*, Schulte Roth & Zabel LLP.

20 C2ES. 2015. *Weathering the Next Storm: A Closer Look at Business Resilience*. Center for Climate and Energy Solutions.

21 Schwartz, P. 2011. *Learnings from the Long View*. Global Business Network.

22 Fulmer, W.E. 2000. *Shaping the Adaptive Organization: Landscapes, Learning, and Leadership in Volatile Times*. New York: Amacom.

23 Hawken, P., J. Ogilvy and P. Schwartz. 1982. *Seven Tomorrows: Toward a Voluntary History*. Covelo, CA: Bantam Books.

24 Schwartz, P. 1996. *The Art of the Long View: Planning for the Future in an Uncertain World*. New York: Doubleday.

25 Wack, P. 1985. Scenarios: Shooting the rapids, *Harvard Business Review*, 63/6: 139–150.

26 Wilkinson, A. and R. Kupers. 2013. Living in the futures, *Harvard Business Review*, 91/5: 118–127.

27 Shell. 2008. *Scenarios: An Explorer's Guide. Exploring the Future*. The Hague: Shell International BV.

28 Schoemaker, P.J.H. 1995. Scenario planning: A tool for strategic thinking, *Sloan Management Review*, 36/2: 25–40.

29 Malaska, P. and I. Virtanen. 2005. Theory of futuribles, *Finnish Future Society. Futura*, 2–3: 5–28.

30 van der Heijden, K. 2005. *Scenarios: The Art of Strategic Conversation*. 2nd edn. Chichester, UK: John Wiley & Sons.

31 Lindgren, M. and H. Bandhold. 2009. *Scenario Planning: The Link Between Future and Strategy*. 2nd edn. Houndmills, UK: Palgrave Macmillan.

32 Chermack, T.J. 2011. *Scenario Planning in Organizations: How to Create, Use, and Assess Scenarios*. Oakland, CA: Berrett-Koehler.

33 Martelli, A. 2014. *Models of Scenario Building and Planning: Facing Uncertainty and Complexity*. Bocconi on Management, ed. R. Grant. Houndmills, UK: Palgrave Macmillan.

34 Wack, P. 1985. Scenarios: Uncharted waters ahead, *Harvard Business Review*, 63/5: 73–89.

35 Schwartz, P. and D. Randall. 2003. *An Abrupt Climate Change Scenario and Its Implications for United States National Security*. Washington.

36 IPCC. 2018. *Global Warming of 1.5°C*. Intergovernmental Panel on Climate Change. http://ipcc.ch/report/sr15/, accessed 13 October 2018.

37 Rigby, D. and B. Bilodeau. 2007. A growing focus on preparedness, *Harvard Business Review*, 85/7/8: 21–22.

38 National Research Council. 2002. *Abrupt Climate Change: Inevitable Surprises*. Washington DC: National Academy Press.

39 Ramírez, R. and A. Wilkinson. 2016. *Strategic Reframing: The Oxford Scenario Planning Approach*. Oxford: Oxford University Press.

40 Schwartz, P. 2003. *Inevitable Surprises: Thinking Ahead in a Time of Turbulence*. New York: Gotham Books.

41 Ceres. 2017. *SEC Sustainability Disclosure Search Tool*. Ceres. https://www.ceres.org/resources/tools/sec-sustainability-disclosure, accessed 27 March 2017.

42 TCFD. 2016. *The Use of Scenario Analysis in Disclosure of Climate-Related Risks and Opportunities*. Financial Stability Board Task Force on Climate-Related Financial Disclosures. https://www.fsb-tcfd.org/publications/technical-supplement/#, accessed 20 Feb 2017.

43 Bazerman, M.H. and M.D. Watkins. 2004. *Predictable Surprises: The Disasters You Should Have Seen Coming, and How to Prevent Them*. Leadership for the Common Good. Boston: Harvard Business School Press.

44 Haigh, N.L. and P. Case. 2015. Firm response to climate change issues with potential for climatic surprise: Preliminary results, Academy of Management Conference. Vancouver.

45 Haigh, N.L. and A. Griffiths. 2012. Surprise as a catalyst for including climatic change in the strategic environment, *Business & Society*, 51/1: 89–120.

46 Ralston, B. and I. Wilson. 2006. *The Scenario-Planning Handbook: A Practitioner's Guide to Developing and Using Scenarios to Direct Strategy in Today's Uncertain Times*. Mason, OH: Thomson/South-Western.

47 Harvard Business School. 2000. Scenario planning reconsidered, *Harvard Management Update*, 5/9: 4.

1

LIMITATIONS OF TRADITIONAL STRATEGIZING AND STRENGTHS OF SCENARIO PLANNING FOR CLIMATE CHANGE

Many companies find themselves dissatisfied with their ability to strategize, because few strategizing techniques are adequate for today's continuously evolving and increasingly turbulent environment. In fact, annual strategic planning processes have been widely panned as ineffective since the 1980s,[1] and more recently Pierre Wack likened the strategic planning process to a "corporate rain dance," where it is performed but often has no influence on subsequent events.[2] Attempts to apply traditional strategizing techniques to climate change and its long-term implications is likely to exacerbate these existing frustrations. Below is a review of the key limitations of rationalist, probabilistic, single-future approaches to strategizing for climate change, and how complementing scenario planning with traditional strategizing can address those limitations.

Limitations of traditional strategizing

Short time horizons

Traditional strategic planning processes typically produce strategic plans with a rolling five-year time horizon. This time horizon may be longer in some sectors, such as forestry, where strategic plans project decades into the future to account for the production cycle of its product; however, five years is considered a norm among many organizations. These shorter five-year strategic plans are important for giving decision-makers a view of what may emerge during their tenure. A five-year strategic plan makes sense when the most popular term of a CEO contract is three or five years.[3] However, a five-year time horizon limits longer-term strategizing that is in the interests of organizational longevity, because it focuses on known trends and competition,[2] and because most significant organizational investments, assets, opportunities, and challenges will outlive it. Many of the challenges and opportunities relating to climate change will also outlive a five-year time horizon.

Scenario planning methods are developed specifically for longer-term strategizing, into which five-year strategic plans should be positioned. Scenario planning helps decision-makers appreciate that long-term decisions are important, and that they are qualitatively different from shorter-term decisions.[2] The appropriate scenario planning time horizon for your organization may be shorter or longer relative to others, but it will typically be longer than a traditional five-year strategic plan, since the purpose of scenario planning is to consider what may be over the horizon. In this book, I focus on a 25-year time horizon. Other time horizons can also be accommodated, but a 25-year time horizon will push your thinking beyond a traditional five-year strategic plan, and is just long enough for the current state of climate science to support your research. Chapter 1 covers what to consider as you determine the best time horizon for your organization.

A single view of the future that avoids uncertainty

Traditional approaches to strategizing often adopt a rational, probabilistic approach that envisions a single (usually desired) future, and develops a strategy to create and then operate successfully within it. Traditional strategies are, after all, driven significantly by the vision of leaders developing them, and leaders are rewarded for being visionary. Real options planning is also a single-view approach, because even though it produces multiple strategic options, they tend to circle around a single potential future.[4] Likewise, risk management is a single-view approach, because it produces a list of more or less probable and impactful risks to which the single view of the future may be exposed.

The problem is that single-view approaches essentially gamble on a single vision of the future actually emerging. As Woody Wade mentioned in his book, *Scenario Planning: A Field Guide to the Future*, "there is no such thing as *the* future."[5] Focusing on a single view of the future creates what Paul Schoemaker at the University of Pennsylvania has called "tunnel vision"[6] by making you blind to other possibilities. What if that single desired future doesn't emerge? Given the dynamic nature of the strategic landscape, coupled with the uncertainty that climate change brings, it seems increasingly unlikely that any single view of the future would emerge. As Pierre Wack[7] stated,

> ... *sooner or later forecasts will fail when they are needed most: in anticipating major shifts in the business environment that make whole strategies obsolete.*

Coupled with relying on a single view of the future, forecasting is often based on previous rates of change and past performance. Even though we live in times where turbulence and rapid change occur regularly, traditional approaches to strategizing often don't consider that rates of change might change.[6] Steady rates of change often only exist in theory, while reality tends to follow uneven rates of change and even punctuated equilibria. The rate of adoption of renewable energy technologies, such as solar photovoltaic (PV) technologies provides an example: The adoption of solar PV technologies can be boosted or interrupted by myriad variables, such as the availability of investment dollars to fund development and commercialization, the implementation or repeal of government subsidies and other incentives, the wholesale price of electricity they produce relative to other renewable and fossil fuel technologies, the emergence of new competing technologies (other renewables), the emergence of new complementary technologies (like battery technologies), changes in market preference for renewable energy, changes in supply from existing technologies, and other variables, all suggesting it is unrealistic to expect a predictable rate of adoption.

Increasing the accuracy of forecasts or rates of change will not improve rational, probabilistic strategizing, because it still relies on a single view of the future. Planning for a single future can only work when all aspects of that future are known and are certain to happen, which is rarely the case. As the above solar PV example illustrates, probabilistic approaches to strategizing are not appropriate amid the uncertainty of today's world, because our economic, social, environmental, and technological systems are too interdependent, too complex, and too uncertain to gamble on a single future.

By helping decision-makers focus on *plausibility* rather than *probability*, and "expecting and examining uncertainty as normal"[4] scenario planning produces more effective strategizing. The word "plausible" in scenario planning is a carefully chosen one that avoids probabilistic predictions and normative declarations, and rather just looks at what *could* happen.[2]

People often ask whether, in economic terms, scenario planning aims to identify possible "black swan events." Black swan events are rare but highly consequential,[5] and therefore usually surprising events that are difficult to predict, because they are outside the realm of normal planning processes. Black swan events are usually negative (e.g. 9/11 attack on the U.S., or the Fukushima disaster in Japan), but can also be positive (e.g. the recent accidental discovery of plastic-eating bacteria, or years ago the discovery of penicillin). By undertaking scenario planning, you will be trying to identify a range of metaphorical swans, some of which may be black, in that it's not a method just to identify impactful events that are difficult to predict, but rather a range of *plausible* impactful events and event combinations. Scenarios will usually include a range of possible outcomes, each of which may be positive or negative, surprising or predictable, sudden or incremental, and be of large or small magnitude, and will facilitate your preparation for whatever unfolds.

By undertaking scenario planning, you overcome the single future problem through a process of identifying driving forces that will shape your organization's future, and developing multiple plausible scenarios based on different combinations of those forces. Scenario planning helps decision-makers prepare for "futures that might happen, rather than the future they would like to create."[2] By understanding how underlying forces beyond your control can shape the future, you can construct multiple scenarios, and develop flexible strategies to prepare for whatever unfolds.

Optimism bias

Another limitation of traditional strategizing is that it is fed by optimism bias. Optimism bias,[8] also known as unrealistic optimism[9] or overconfidence,[6, 10] is a deep-rooted and pervasive cognitive bias affecting most people. Cognitive neuroscientist Tali Sharot defines optimism bias as a "cognitive illusion" where we tend to "overestimate our likelihood of experiencing good events and underestimate the likelihood of experiencing bad events" relative to actual probabilities of them being experienced by the average person or society as a whole.[11] Sharot found that those parts of the brain which monitor emotional salience – the amygdala and rostral anterior cingulate cortex – become more highly activated when people imagine positive future events and are less activated when they imagine negative future events;[8] leading us to see the world through rose-tinted glasses. We each assume that we possess unique capabilities that will ensure things turn out for the good, and use this belief to furnish the details of an uncertain future.[12]

The implication of optimism bias is that we don't give enough weight to the possibility of negative outcomes, especially when there are considerable potential benefits in the good outcomes.[13] This relates to the single view problem: Focusing on one desired future prevents us from taking precautionary action to avoid or adequately limit our exposure to other possible (or even probable) less appealing futures. In business settings, research has found that optimism bias manifests as projects over-running their anticipated time, cost, and scope,[14] inability to kill failing projects,[15] inaccurate projections of organizational performance,[10] and markets and investments not performing as well as anticipated.[16, 17] Joan Costa-Font and his colleagues at the London School of Economics found optimism bias present in relation to climate change.[13] True to form, Costa-Font found that people perceived that climate change would affect society as a whole more than it would affect them personally.

In her 2012 TED Talk, Tali Sharot said that to manage optimism bias "we need to be able to imagine a different reality, and then we need to believe that that reality is possible."[11] Scenario planning helps to manage optimism bias in several ways. It facilitates the identification of real forces that are driving plausible long-term futures, some of which will be uncomfortable to consider, and others that will be pleasant. It also weights each scenario equally, so that one "preferred future" scenario cannot be chosen over others.

However, being aware of optimism bias does not address it, and while scenario planning helps to manage it, optimism bias also needs to be managed within the scenario planning process. For instance, research at the University of Pennsylvania found that optimism bias can affect scenario planning.[6] Nearly 60 MBA students were asked to develop positive and negative scenarios for the industry in which they expected to work after graduation. Students scored each underlying trend driving their scenarios according to whether it was positive, negative, or indeterminate, and identified only 1.48 negative trends to every 2 positive trends – they believed positive outcomes were more probable than negative outcomes. To manage optimism bias within the scenario planning process, it is important to foster and accommodate diverse views, and not to aim for consensus. Not requiring consensus is a strength of scenario planning and is discussed more below.

To conclude these major limitations, continuing to only develop five-year strategic plans for a single, desired future – into which the life of most significant investments would not fit – is risky, and is likely the reason that few strategies are actually implemented as written. Applying only a five-year strategic plan to climate change without also engaging in longer-term strategizing is increasingly dangerous.

Strengths of scenario planning

Scenario planning is not as static as, nor has the gambling element of, traditional single-view strategizing, and it will deepen your appreciation of how limited much of our thinking is. In addition to the ways that scenario planning addresses the limitations of traditional strategizing for climate change, it has several other strengths.

Challenges assumptions

Scenario planning can be confronting, because it challenges the conventional wisdom of strategizing based on known trends and competition. Scenario planning presents decision-makers with plausible inconvenient truths (as Al Gore might put it) about trends that are currently just out of view but could put an organization into counter-intuitive or unsettling situations.

Thinking about uncomfortable situations and uncertainties is at odds with our optimism bias, and while this is one of the strengths of scenario planning, it can lead first-timers to question its usefulness. Thinking about uncertainties can leave senior decision-makers feeling extremely uncomfortable, insecure, and even untethered,[18] because it questions the good judgement that got them to their current position. Executives in this position may believe scenario planning is not helpful, because they trust their own judgement, and scenarios present uncertainties over which they have no control and no ability to exercise that judgment.[4] In his book *The Art of the Long View,* Peter Schwartz recalled instances where his scenario planning efforts were ridiculed for being too "implausible." People in my own workshops and classes have explicitly demonstrated their discomfort by saying "I don't want to think about that!" when presented with uncomfortable scenarios. I have also heard people try to dismiss large issues (like a flood that would affect an entire community) by saying: "Well, if that happens, we'll all be affected" as if this were a reason to do nothing. These are all signs that scenarios are challenging the foundations of "business-as-usual" assumptions.[19] People often ignore uncertainties or attempt to reduce them to a simplified view of the world that accords with their "mental map" of the future.[18] This mental map assumes what is important about the future, and what decisions are priorities. In reality, it is these uncertainties over which no control or judgment can be exercised that should command most strategizing attention.

We often don't realize we have an assumption until it is challenged or compared with the assumptions of others.[18] In scenario planning discussions, strong emotions and differences can come to the fore, and you will know that someone's assumptions are being unearthed when critical questions are asked, or when someone is challenging, denying, or dismissing particular scenarios or the method generally. Examples of assumptions might include assuming that a commodity will continue to be available (or available within a certain price range), that a current technology will still be relevant, or that the physical environment including climate will remain much the same. By identifying forces that will shape your organization's future and using them to develop scenarios, scenario planning presents situations that cannot be resolved using these kinds of assumptions, because they may not be adequate in times of great unfamiliarity or crisis. As you begin to work through the scenario planning method, be prepared to "thoroughly review your mental maps of the world, question your assumptions and challenge comfortable perceptions,"[18] and build new mental maps, as described below.

Builds new integrative mental models of the future that embrace uncertainty

Pierre Wack argued, that "exposing and invalidating an obsolete worldview is not where scenario analysis stops. Reconstructing a new model is the most important job."[7] We each carry powerful mental models and perceptions that, as Hawken, Ogilvy and Schwartz noted from their experience, "guide actions as much if not more than facts."[20] Alex Metzger, a recent PhD graduate of the University of Massachusetts Boston, who has done extensive research into mental models about flooding in Boston, gives some of its history in his doctoral dissertation:[21]

> Craik (1943) coined the concept mental models as each individual's unique internal representation of external reality, underlying reasoning, perception, and decision-making ... Mental models provide a basis for understanding stakeholder values, beliefs, and decision-making strategies and contain local expert and traditional knowledge about complex social-ecological system dynamics (Biggs et al. 2011; Manfredo et al. 2014; Gray et al. 2012; Doyle and Ford 1998). Mental model diversity, when integrated into decision making and management ... can provide a robust basis for adaptation to changing conditions or understandings ...

Constructing new mental models (others' and yours) through scenario planning takes time and effort, because it requires decision-makers to engage with data on a deeper level than they may desire, and to embrace uncertainty. The time and effort invested is important to what Adam Kahane describes as "transforming understandings," so you can come to see a situation and your role in it with fresh eyes.[22] If you are accustomed to relying on macroeconomic analytical reports, industry reports, commodity projections, and other types of forecasts produced by others (either in-house or by third parties), then scenario planning may seem like an onerous task that someone else should do. Nothing could be further from the truth. While you should use these reports and available administrative resources to collect data, confirm trends, and undertake some of the preliminary analyses, you will need to do enough of your own research to draw your own conclusions about the driving forces and scenarios, so you can discuss them authoritatively, in depth. This research, and discussion of insights from it among peers, is how new mental models are built, and good strategies are developed.

The new mental models you build will be more integrative, which will give you a better view of the dynamics of the world around the organization, and enable you to identify a wider array of risks, opportunities, and threats, and reduce your vulnerability to surprises.[23] The new capabilities and knowledge created during the process will become a powerful asset for you and your organization.

You should approach the method knowing that others have gone before you and that they are telling you there is light at the end of the tunnel, because once you have developed options to deal with your worst case scenario (i.e. a surrogate crisis[24]), you will likely (and rightly) feel calm, uplifted and accomplished. The process has been described as:

> *Elation, information overload, disorientation surrounding too many scenario ideas and lack of clarity about how to use them, and then back to elation once the future is seen with fresh eyes.*[18]

To change mental models, scenario planning relies on improvisation, creativity, innovation,[18] and organizational learning.[2] Even after more than thirty years of being a scenario planning pioneer, Shell continues to learn from the process.[18]

Being in the thick of improvisation can be disorienting for anyone who is task-oriented and ends meetings with concrete decisions that have emerged from consensus or majority vote. If/When you feel disoriented or overwhelmed, or are questioning scenario planning as a useful method for strategizing, or the time and effort required, I challenge you to keep working through it at least until you develop strategic options for your worst case scenario. By then you will have become more effective as a leader by gaining a richer view of your organization and the forces shaping its future, and you will have developed options that could mean the difference between successful and failed responses.[18] The value of scenario planning should be obvious to you at that point.

Does not require consensus

Another strength of scenario planning is that scenarios are plausible stories, not official positions or outlooks that require everyone's agreement. The aim of scenario planning is not a single agreed-upon future, but to consider multiple different plausible futures. Scenario planning has been said to create "a 'safe space' in which more and different perspectives can be revealed, and alternative frames compared, to generate new and shared understanding to test and develop options for action."[25]

Using the method set out in this book, you will develop four scenarios. Each scenario will be qualitatively different from the others, because each will be driven by a different combination of underlying forces and their collective impacts on the organization, and other dynamics within its strategic landscape given that combination. Some of the scenarios will likely have favorable outcomes, while others will likely have unfavorable outcomes. The set of scenarios you develop should become a sampler, if you will, of plausible futures. The scenarios will be treated as equally probable – identifying a preferred scenario is not only unnecessary, it also reduces the effectiveness of the method.

On a more interpersonal level, scenario planning works best if it is approached with a sense of adventure and fun,[18] since some of the scenarios you develop, the names you give them, and especially the discussions around them, can provide some comic relief! As Wilkinson and Kupers put it in their Harvard Business Review article, scenario planning encourages "a healthy exchange of differing perspectives."[2] It's important that the differing perspectives are allowed to come to the surface, and that people be able to support or challenge them. If you can maintain a supportive and playful environment for those discussions without requiring consensus, the process will be more engaging for everyone, and more effective.

In my experience, one area where divergent views about climate change often emerge is whether, and if so then how and to what degree, national policies will curb carbon emissions. From one perspective, the ratification of the Kyoto Protocol in 2005, implementation of the European Union Emission Trading System, and continuing talks at Conferences of the Parties indicate a global shift towards regulating and reducing carbon emissions. However, the policy initiatives of each signatory country can change as administrations change (e.g. introducing or repealing carbon policy; both of which have occurred in Australia, and countries entering or exiting international treaties; both of which the U.S. did with the Paris Climate Accord). At a more granular level, states and cities have also implemented their own carbon reduction initiatives. Added to this, as mentioned earlier, large companies (especially energy companies) lobby policymakers at city, state, and national levels, and this influences the timing, longevity, and content of carbon policies. Further to this already substantial variability, as decision-makers consider how these all affect their organization (or not), people bring their own personal and professional training and beliefs, and optimism bias, to discussions of carbon policy, and this can lead them to focus on what they believe *should* occur in future, rather than determine what *could plausibly* occur in future. The result can be extreme uncertainty, since carbon policy, the lack of it, and other situations in between all become plausible. Scenario planning can accommodate these possibilities in separate scenarios, where the diverse views can be explored without the need for consensus.

An added bonus of not requiring consensus is that it helps to manage "group think"[18] by encouraging alternate views, and discouraging simply agreeing with the more powerful people in the room. Scenario planning efforts must still attend to power relationships to ensure the method is carried out ethically,[25] and if attention is paid to ethics, it can create a safe and innovative space to discuss and contest ideas about the future that go far beyond what has been called "the incremental, comfortable, and familiar progression customary in a consensus culture."[2] In this space, you and other decision-makers can (without pulling rank) make your cases for what is plausible, but accept there will diverse viewpoints, that not everyone will agree with you, and that lack of consensus can remain. The benefit of accommodating diverse views is that it keep communication lines open to informal and formal cross-fertilization of ideas in meetings, workshops, and perhaps more importantly in side conversations that take place after meetings.

So, approach the lack of consensus with a sense of adventure and play – humor is a great tool to disarm people whose mental models might be very stubborn, or who might fear the process will undermine any role they had in setting the current strategic plan, or if the organization does not have a culture that is open to diverse points of view. People will be less likely to be defensive and more likely to be open if the process inspires everyone's creativity, resourcefulness and imagination.

Builds strategic flexibility and timing

The TCFD argued that focusing on multiple potential climate change scenarios enables decision-makers to develop flexible and rigorous climate change strategies.[19] Flexibility is key to responding successfully to uncertainty and unforeseen change, and therefore is crucial to successful strategizing.[26] The need for flexibility is increasingly important given that organizations often do not respond to climate change until they are directly affected; that is, when the crisis is already upon them.[27, 28] Scenario planning enables organizations to become more flexible in their strategizing and in their strategies, which builds resilience, and helps to respond quickly when crisis strikes.[23]

In particular, companies in industries where technological, product, and markets move quickly can benefit from scenario planning, since increasing flexibility enables them to reduce the negative impacts of a change, and to increase their response capacity. By considering multiple future scenarios far in advance of their potential emergence, and by identifying warning signals, scenario planning gives organizations more time to anticipate potential upcoming changes, and to develop a variety of cost-effective options to be implemented if and when needed. In this sense, scenario planning develops a keen sense of strategic timing that will enable you to stay ahead of emerging change, stay ahead of competitors, and decide when and how to respond. If you can relate to this statement by Harvard Business School – "if you wait for a trend to be validated … the window of opportunity will have closed or the threat will have already torpedoed your company"[1] – then scenario planning can help you to identify trends well ahead of their emergence, and enable you to get ahead of upcoming threats and opportunities by timing your response.

In conclusion, a stand-alone five-year strategic planning process focused on a single view of the future is ineffective, and complementing it with scenario planning will help to overcome its limitations, while building valuable in-house capabilities to strategize rigorously and flexibly for the long term.

References

1 Harvard Business School. 2000. Scenario planning reconsidered, *Harvard Management Update*, 5/9: 4.
2 Wilkinson, A. and R. Kupers. 2013. Living in the futures, *Harvard Business Review*, 91/5: 118–127.
3 Schwab, S.J. and R.S. Thomas. 2006. An empirical analysis of CEO employment contracts: What do top executives bargain for, *Washington and Lee Law Review*, 63: 231–270.
4 Wack, P. 1985. Scenarios: Shooting the rapids, *Harvard Business Review*, 63/6: 139–150.
5 Wade, W. 2012. *Scenario Planning: A Field Guide to the Future*. Hoboken, USA: John Wiley & Sons.
6 Schoemaker, P.J.H. 1995. Scenario planning: A tool for strategic thinking, *Sloan Management Review*, 36/2: 25–40.
7 Wack, P. 1985. Scenarios: Uncharted waters ahead, *Harvard Business Review*, 63/5: 73–89.
8 Sharot, T., A.M. Riccardi, C.M. Raio and E.A. Phelps. 2007. Neural mechanisms mediating optimism bias, *Nature*, 450/7166: 102–105.
9 Weinstein, N.D. 1980. Unrealistic optimism about future life events, *Journal of Personality and Social Psychology*, 39/5: 806–820.
10 Libby, R. and K.M. Rennekamp. 2016. Experienced financial managers' views of the relationships among self-serving attribution bias, overconfidence, and the issuance of management forecasts: A replication, *Journal of Financial Reporting*, 1/1: 131–136.
11 Sharot, T. 2012. Tali Sharot: The optimism bias. *TED*. http://www.ted.com/talks/tali_sharot_the_optimism_bias#t-1008491, accessed 2 February 2017.
12 Heyman, B. 1998. Introduction, in *Risk, Health and Health Care*, ed. B. Heyman, London: Arnold. pp. 1–23.
13 Costa-Font, J., E. Mossialos and C. Rudisill. 2009. Optimism and the perceptions of new risks, *Journal of Risk Research*, 12/1: 27–41.
14 Son, J. and E.M. Rojas. 2010. Impact of optimism bias regarding organizational dynamics on project planning and control, *Journal of Construction Engineering and Management*, 137/2: 147–157.
15 Meyer, W.G. 2014. The effect of optimism bias on the decision to terminate failing projects, *Project Management Journal*, 45/4: 7–20.
16 Wang, J., X. Wang, X. Zhuang and J. Yang. 2017. Optimism bias, portfolio delegation, and economic welfare, *Economics Letters*, 150: 111–113.
17 Rajapakse, S. and M. Siriwardana. 2007. Over-optimism bias in market analysts' forecasts: The case of the Australian dollar, *Journal of the Asia Pacific Economy*, 12/1: 103–113.
18 Shell. 2008. *Scenarios: An Explorer's Guide. Exploring the Future*. The Hague: Shell International BV.
19 TCFD. 2016. *The Use of Scenario Analysis in Disclosure of Climate-Related Risks and Opportunities*. Financial Stability Board Task Force on Climate-Related Financial Disclosures. https://www.fsb-tcfd.org/publications/technical-supplement/#, accessed 20 Feb 2017.
20 Hawken, P., J. Ogilvy and P. Schwartz. 1982. *Seven Tomorrows: Toward a Voluntary History*. Covelo, CA: Bantam Books.

21 Metzger, A. 2018. *Models That Matter: Using Novel Participatory Modeling Methods to Integrate Mental Models into an Adaptive Co-management Process.* PhD thesis, School for the Environment, University of Massachusetts Boston: Boston.

22 Kahane, A. 2012. *Transformative Scenario Planning: Working Together to Change the Future.* San Francisco: Berrett-Koehler.

23 Ralston, B. and I. Wilson. 2006. *The Scenario-Planning Handbook: A Practitioner's Guide to Developing and Using Scenarios to Direct Strategy in Today's Uncertain Times.* Mason, OH: Thomson/South-Western.

24 Schoemaker, P.J.H. 1998. Twenty common pitfalls in scenario planning, in *Learning from the Future: Competitive Foresight Scenarios*, ed. L. Fahey and R.M. Randall. New York: John Wiley & Sons. pp. 422–431.

25 Ramírez, R. and A. Wilkinson. 2016. *Strategic Reframing: The Oxford Scenario Planning Approach.* Oxford: Oxford University Press.

26 Eppink, D.J. 1978. Planning for strategic flexibility, *Long Range Planning*, 11/4: 9–15.

27 Haigh, N.L. and A. Griffiths. 2012. Surprise as a catalyst for including climatic change in the strategic environment, *Business & Society*, 51/1: 89–120.

28 Haigh, N.L. and P. Case. 2015. Firm response to climate change issues with potential for climatic surprise: Preliminary results. Academy of Management Conference. Vancouver.

2

STEP 1: SET THE AGENDA, FOCAL QUESTION, AND TIME HORIZON, AND IDENTIFY KEY STAKEHOLDERS

Step 1 comprises four sub-steps that will establish your scenario planning project: Setting the agenda and identifying internal stakeholders, defining the focal question, defining an appropriate time horizon, and identifying key external stakeholders. This is the first point at which you may experience some iteration, as people brought into the project will influence the agenda, question, and time horizon, while defining the question and time horizon may necessitate revisiting who is involved in the project. In addition to covering the sub-steps outlined above, this step will facilitate convening a scenario planning project team, and developing a scenario planning project plan.

Set the agenda and identify key internal stakeholders

Setting the agenda includes answering initial questions about the rationale for undertaking scenario planning, who should champion the project within your organization, who will be the project manager, which internal (and possibly also external) people should be on the team, and what will be the project's expected duration and budget? It is necessary to have these people and decisions in place before embarking on Step 2, to ensure the initial project structure is established and all necessary people are included.

As you go through the process of starting the project, document everything you do. A working project document can become a dynamic, living document that describes the project, its audience, and the rationale for undertaking it, and as the project proceeds, this early document can provide an excellent basis for recording the process and decisions made along the way, and ultimately reporting on the project and its outcomes.

The first project documents should be a proposal for the scenario planning project, and a presentation. In these early stages, starting a proposal and presentation will help you explain the purpose of the project to relevant senior stakeholders, and potential champions, and address any questions or concerns they may have.[1, 2] It'll also give you a place to start listing potential team members and making notes. In his book *Scenario Planning in Organizations*,[3] Thomas Chermack provides an excellent example of a sample scenario project proposal that includes sections outlining the purpose of the project, estimated scope and time frame (including a broad timeline mapping out workshops and meetings), team members and roles, general expected outcomes, project measurements including estimated costs and benefits, and how the success of the project would be measured. You can download a generic sample project proposal (with notes) for a climate change scenario planning project at www.nardiahaigh.com.

The proposal will become the basis for making the case to get the project up and running (communicating what will be done, when, and the budget and other resources required), and as the project proceeds, other project documents will record how the method was carried out, track key milestones, as well as describing assumptions, drivers, scenarios, warning signals, recommended strategic options, and feedback received.

Below are some of the questions on which you will need clarity as you build the proposal for your own scenario planning project, and put a team together. Having these questions answered before you begin will help you make a case for starting the project, and help you answer questions from people who may be disinterested, be focusing on costs, or be detractors. Having a good idea of your rationale for the scenario planning project and its intended outcomes will also help you to answer other project-related questions as you proceed, and will inform good choices about other important aspects of the project.[4]

Why should we undertake scenario planning, and what outcomes do we seek?

Very little progress will be made without a detailed understanding why your organization should undertake scenario planning. In his book, *Transformative Scenario Planning: Working Together to Change the Future*, Adam Kahane[5] described a general reason that might have brought you to the idea of scenario planning:

> You look at what is going on in your community or sector or region, and you are not content with what you see. You see possible futures that you are not willing to accept because they continue an unacceptable present, destroy an acceptable present, or fail to realize the potential of the present. And you are not willing to leave what will happen to chance or to others. You want to contribute to creating a better future.

Whatever case you build for scenario planning, Ralston and Wilson[6] suggest keeping your agenda a simple one that sets out uncertainties (in this case, climate change uncertainties), shows how scenario planning can be used to address them, and points out potential risks of not engaging scenario planning to address the uncertainties.

There is an intuitive rationale built into this book that standard five-year strategic planning is not sufficient to strategize for climate change, and that decision-makers should, as a matter of responsible long-term strategizing and decision-making, understand how climate change could plausibly affect their organizations. Several intended outcomes are also built into the book: The development of long-term climate change strategies that will build organizational flexibility around climate change, and integrate climate change and scenario planning into the organization's strategic planning process. You may have the same or different rationale and intended outcomes, and they will likely develop further as you put the team together and the project begins.

What specific outcomes do we seek?

It is worthwhile skipping ahead to read the Chapter 5 section on assessing scenario planning projects before you document the specific outcomes you seek, so you can develop outcomes that are specific and measurable.

Taking the time to articulate specific outcomes will help the project stay on track, help you weigh the intended outcomes against the projected costs of the project, and provide you with baselines for post-project assessment. It will also help you to manage expectations within the team and the broader organization. Below are some example outcomes that you might seek from a scenario planning project focusing on climate change that may be useful for brainstorming purposes:

- Greater knowledge about climate change and how it may affect the organization, by decision-makers, team members, key stakeholders, and the organization more broadly
- Increased capacity for climate change adaptation concerning a specific climate change issue, such as flooding, drought, policy changes, or extreme weather
- Improved decision-making that takes climate change impacts into account, including better risk management and business continuity
- Enhanced ability to engage in climate change conversations held locally, regionally, nationally, or in your industry
- Updating existing strategic planning processes to incorporate climate change and/or scenario planning
- Improved medium and long-term operations performance, which may include existing operational measures (such as goods/services produced, new products developed, product quality, employee satisfaction, safety, etc.)
- Improved medium and long-term financial performance (revenue, costs, profit, cash, etc., and various ratios)
- Development of new performance measures (e.g. estimated savings created by adaptation strategies, insurance claims or operational disruptions avoided due to anticipating extreme weather, or drought-related supply disruptions avoided by identifying additional suppliers in different locations)

Will scenario planning be integrated with organizational strategic planning, or will it be a stand-alone project?

Once you have a sense of broad outcomes you'd like to achieve through scenario planning, it's important to know at this early stage whether your efforts will be stand-alone or integrated into strategic planning, because it will influence the project agenda, timelines, scope, choice of team members, project manager, budget, among other things, and determine whether your scenario planning efforts produce strategies, or recommendations for those responsible for strategic planning.

If there is one glaring problem with scenario planning, it's that in many instances, it is designed to be done outside the regular strategic planning process. This problem was recognized by Liam Fahey and Robert Randall back in 1998 in their edited book, *Learning from the Future: Competitive Foresight Scenarios.*[7] Fahey and Randall argued, that "[t]o become truly useful to an organization, scenario learning should be directly integrated with its strategy analysis frameworks and processes."[7] Added to this, in his chapter in the same book on the pitfalls of scenario planning, Paul Schoemaker noted that failing to connect scenario planning efforts with strategic planning efforts is a key but avoidable mistake.[8] Since 1998, more people practicing and writing about scenario planning have started to link it with strategic planning; though there is still work to be done, perhaps because of conflicts perceived in time horizons, single vs. multiple futures, a focus on probability over plausibility, or perhaps because scenario planning may not need to be done every year, as strategic planning often is.

The TCFD explicitly advises companies to "apply scenario analysis as part of their strategic planning and/or enterprise risk management processes" to ensure they understand their "future potential exposure to climate-related transition and physical risks (and opportunities)," to evaluate "the potential effects on their strategic and financial position under each of the defined scenarios," and use "the results to identify options for managing the identified risks and opportunities through adjustments to strategic and financial plans."[2]

In their book, Fahey and Randall[7] wrote a chapter on integrating strategy and scenarios. Using their work as a basis, below are several connections between scenario planning and strategic planning, related to climate change, using as an example the Okanagan Valley farmers mentioned in the Introduction:

- Ideas for new products, new markets, new customers, and new competitors can emerge from your scenarios. Okanagan Valley businesses found a new product in wine on account of rising temperatures and shorter winters.
- Ideas for new ways of competing can emerge from your scenarios. At a basic level, organizations compete on the basis of price, differentiation, or both, and within markets that are broadly or narrowly defined. Okanagan Valley businesses were able to move from a portfolio of milk and apple cost-based commodity products, and introduce wine as a differentiated product.

- Scenarios can affect the goals, vision, and mission of an organization. While there is no documentation, it's evident that Okanagan Valley businesses changed their goals, vision, and mission to include wine production.
- The scenario planning method can improve strategic management processes to understand the driving forces in the strategic landscape, to identify, develop, and choose among strategic options. While there is no documentation, Okanagan Valley businesses would need to tune their strategic management processes to include the wine production cycle, and the temperature, precipitation, and seasonal marketing norms that drive wine production, distribution, and consumption.
- The scenario planning method can improve processes to execute strategies. For instance, the flexibility gained through scenario planning can help you alter the timing a particular strategy will be executed – such as relocating a plant – well ahead of time, if tracked warning signals (e.g. sea level change) indicate it may be prudent to do so. While there is no evidence scenario planning was undertaken, it's evident that Okanagan Valley businesses showed exceptional long-term planning skills and executed it at the appropriate time, allowing them to drive up the value of their land as a primary capital asset.

The method covered in this book accommodates scenario planning efforts that will generate recommendations or strategies, and recognizes that you may be undertaking scenario planning as a stand-alone project, especially if the organization has never done scenario planning before. If you are generating recommendations as a stand-alone project, and like some other scenario planners, are concerned that your scenarios may not result in "nothing more than interesting speculation,"[9] have a goal of integrating it into strategic planning next time, and in the meantime, ensure people involved in strategic planning are on the team.

Who will champion the project?

Many scenario planning projects are identified not by the CEO, President, or Chair of the Board, but by other people working in the organization, who will need to identify a champion to support the project, both in principal and by allocating to it money, employee time, and other resources such as space (physical or digital), hardware, or transport. Even if you are the CEO or President, your scenario planning project would benefit by having another senior person (perhaps the Chair of the Board) onboard as a champion. As the project progresses, the champion can support your efforts to complement scenario planning with existing strategic planning processes, so it will become the norm to perform both short-term and long-term strategizing. The champion may be inside or outside your organization depending on your situation, and as Shell[1] noted, may not necessarily be the recipient of the scenarios.

Interviews to identify an internal champion and team members

If you are seeking an internal champion, consider interviewing key decision-makers to determine potential support for a scenario planning project. In these interviews, scenario planners often underscore the need for scenario planning to identify the concerns of key decision-makers.[4]

Interviews can cover wide-ranging topics, including current organizational goals and strategies, broad concerns people have about the organization, and can help identify any thoughts and concerns they have relating specifically to climate change. These meetings will help you learn who sees climate change as a priority (or not), and give you some initial insights into peoples' mental models of how climate change could affect the organization. The interviews will also help you determine who would make good members of the scenario planning team, help define the focal question (covered further below) and uncover initial insights about potential climate drivers (covered in the next chapter).

Your aim is to record each person's views and experiences (especially specific climate issues they see as important, and why). Starting questions might include those listed below. Conducting interviews with mostly open questions will help you access interviewees' perceptions about climate change and as it relates to the organization. Add, delete or edit any of these questions as you see fit:

- What are the organization's main goals over the medium to long-term?

    a   What needs to happen to achieve those goals?
    b   What challenges do you see the organization facing as it works towards those goals?

- Do you think it possible that climate change could affect the organization in future?

    a   How might the organization have been affected by climate in the past?
    b   What climate change issues do you think could affect the organization in future?
    c   What risks or opportunities do you think climate change could bring for the organization?

- Do you see climate change as something the organization should think about within its medium to long-term strategic planning?

Record the interviews where possible, or take notes, because interviewees will give you good insights into their thinking, especially about general challenges and uncertainties the organization may face. Another reason to record the interviews is so you can analyze them to identify themes in the responses, where multiple people make similar comments, raise similar concerns, and make similar statements. Response themes will provide important input into defining the focal question and identifying potential climate change drivers. If you want to dive more deeply into interviewing techniques for scenario planning, Kees van der Heijden[4] provides a good overview in his book, *Scenarios: The Art of Strategic Conversation*.

Who will be the project manager?

The success of the project will depend in large measure on the ability of its leader, who will be responsible for managing the overall process, engaging stakeholders, communicating progress, circulating the results, and assessing the project. If the project will produce strategies and not just recommendations, this person would ideally be a senior person responsible for strategy or planning.[2] If the project will produce recommendations for those who do the strategic planning, then take Bill Ralston and Ian Wilson's advice, and find someone who is "a committed generalist who is knowledgeable about the decision areas, familiar with the company's business and culture, and credible to both senior management and staff."[6]

The position description of the project manager is a demanding one. To deliver the project successfully, the project manager needs to be a competent and respected collaborative leader, who has the authority to manage the budget and team, while also possessing abilities on the creative side of scenario planning. They need to take collaborative responsibility for defining the question and time horizon, synthesizing the team's work at necessary points (such as when ranking the drivers, or developing each scenario), and developing strategic options or recommendations. The combination of organization, leadership, synthesis, and creative skills is important. In particular, Shell[1] argues that this person "must ensure a balance between unconventional thinking and plausibility" as scenarios are considered, so that experts can apply their knowledge to ideas without drowning out creative exploration of them.

The project manager does not need to have expertise in climate change. Further, while prior experience in scenario planning would be beneficial, if that's not the case, consider hiring an experienced scenario planning consultant who can help facilitate the process and act as a mentor to the project manager. If the budget doesn't stretch that far, invest extra time for the project manager to take a course in scenario planning that includes completing an individual scenario planning project, or to learn more about it using books, blogs, and other resources (many of which are referred to throughout this book).

What is the project duration and budget?

The length and budget of scenario planning projects is unique to each organization. Conversations, workshops, and meetings required to undertake scenario planning successfully take time to put together from a logistical standpoint, but more importantly, the content of the gatherings – the ideas that emerge about climate change, driving forces, scenarios, strategic options, etc. – need time to develop.

Peter Schwartz[10] advised from his depth of experience that conversations need to take place regularly (perhaps every two weeks) for up to half a day each, over a period three to nine months. In their book *The Scenario-Planning Handbook: A*

Practitioner's Guide to Developing and Using Scenarios to Direct Strategy in Today's Uncertain Times, Bill Ralston and Ian Wilson estimate that small projects may take up to one month, while larger projects up to six months.[6] In my own teaching, executives or student teams choose a company to study (often their employer), and I take them through the method over a series of classes; during which they go through the entire method and produce a draft scenario planning report (or mock report) that includes strategic options or recommendations.

While it is important that the project keeps moving and results are delivered, if you believe more time may be required at certain points, to let ideas percolate or have additional conversations, consider building in some time buffers so the process can be slowed down temporarily to accommodate these needs. This may create budgetary tension, because people's time is generally the biggest cost in scenario planning, but it will pay off in the end with a more successful project by having everyone engaged (and nobody left behind).

Your project may require more or less time than the 1–6 month times noted above. Start by estimating the time required for each step of the method detailed in this book, then add extra time for contingencies (a significant amount of time if you are currently inexperienced with scenario planning) to avoid budgetary tension (or at least keep it to a minimum).

As you read through the method you will develop a list of budget items; however, a starting list could include:

- Time of all team members and champions
- Time of anyone supporting the project administratively
- Time of anyone reviewing the scenarios
- Facilities and catering required for meetings and workshops
- Travel required for meetings and workshops
- Costs of any external facilitators, experts, consultants, or researchers
- Office supplies and other incidental costs

On a logistical note, with people's time being a significant element of the timeline and budget, start giving thought now to the design and timeline of your project, and start asking questions like: Who should be involved? This is discussed next. When would meetings need to occur? How much notice will people need? Is there a time of year when all (or most) team members are in the office? How long would meetings/ workshops need to take? They can take several days. Do we need an external facilitator? You probably do if it's your first scenario planning project. Do you need to include time to build the team? After you have answered these questions, go back and make any necessary amendments to your proposed timeline and budget.

Who should be on the scenario planning team?

The success of your scenario planning project also depends on the scenario planning team.[5] The question of who should be involved in the scenario planning project will depend on your organization's particular needs, and is a question that can take more time than expected to answer depending on the size of the organization. Ideally, you will avoid taking too long. Elahi and Ramírez[11] noted in their case study of the European Patent Office that selecting participants took three months. Hopefully you won't need that long, else the project risks losing steam before it gets started; however, time is needed to interview potential team members to understand what each person might bring to the project (or detract from it), why they might want to be involved (or not), and how they might interact with other potential team members.[4] As you recruit team members, provide each potential member with a description of the project (perhaps the project proposal, or other scoping document) so you have a basis for discussion.

The scenario planning team may be a small or large, and suggested sizes range from six to 15 to 20 or even 30,[1, 12, 13] and you will need a team of people who are available for the duration of the project (to avoid disruption). Aside from being available, Peter Schwartz[10] gave three guidelines for selecting team members: 1) Gain support for the team from the highest levels of management; 2) Have representation from a wide range of divisions and functions; and 3) Target imaginative people who work well in teams. Each of these is discussed in more detail below.

Gain support for the team from the highest levels of management

Scenario planning produces organizational evolution that requires change management; therefore, all key decision-makers including the executive suite and CEO (or equivalent title) and key board members should be on the team from the beginning, and should be supportive of the team configuration. Not gaining this support at the earliest stages of the project has been identified as a common mistake leading to the downfall of scenario planning projects. The only way to avoid it is to ensure the senior decision-makers are included on the team from the beginning.[8] As Woody Wade mentioned, "… you cannot afford to have participants whom the others don't find credible, or whose contribution to the various discussions will already be discounted before they even open their mouths."[13] The interviews conducted to identify internal champions can also help to identify valuable team members.

Another reason for comprising the scenario team of the organization's leadership is that scenario planning requires in-depth knowledge about the organization's business model, assets, and operations and their geophysical environments, organizational structure, strategic positioning, mission and vision for its future, key stakeholders, markets, brand, and identity. Such knowledge is required in every step of the method, since it will help to identify stakeholders, identify meaningful climate change driving forces, understand how they might affect the organization, and develop meaningful and relevant scenarios, recommendations, or strategies.

In particular, understanding how climate change will affect an organization and how the organization might respond demands detailed knowledge of capital assets and their geographic context, finances, operations, and logistics. Ideally, these decision-makers will be intuitive, and have the sense of adventure and curiosity to embrace the ambiguity that comes with thinking about plausible futures, but if these qualities are lacking within your particular group, then consider adding someone else who has these qualities and is seen as a leader or potential leader within the organization.

Have representation from a wide range of divisions and functions

Beyond the core team of senior people, consider who else in the organization needs to be involved. Schoemaker's[12] research suggests that the whole organization need not be involved in your scenario planning process (he found that scenarios had the same impact regardless of whether they were developed by his research subjects or if subjects were provided with scenarios developed by others). However, inclusiveness and openness are generally beneficial, and will facilitate buy-in, so be sure to involve representatives from front-line customer support, operational employees, and line managers; whether it be in core project team roles, or in supporting roles. This will also spread the workload and maximize the perspectives involved. If this isn't feasible, or your organization is large or too complex, then involve as many people as makes sense.

Start with relevant key people from across the organization's functions, units, or departments, who understand the organization well and hold institutional knowledge and history. Include internal subject matter experts, people who know something about climate change (or perhaps sustainability broadly), and include open-minded imaginative people that will assist the scenario development effort. Other people might include internal research assistants to help the research efforts to identify and analyze driving forces. Include a broad-enough range of people to facilitate buy-in and make the outputs of the process more rigorous and relevant.

Not having diversity in perspectives on the team is another common error people make on scenario planning projects.[8] Create a balance of people from different professional backgrounds; including some who are analytically quantitative and others who are analytically qualitative, so you are able to engage in the qualitative parts of scenario construction, as well as quantifying parts where necessary.

You may also want to include external stakeholders in the process, such as key customers or suppliers, or particular experts. Given that climate change may affect public infrastructure, services, or land, which in turn may affect you or your external stakeholders, it may also be appropriate to involve regulators and local planning authorities. Other outside experts, such as scientists and thought leaders may also prove helpful to bring different perspectives or avoid "institutional myopia."[4]

Target imaginative people who work well in teams

People who are unable or unwilling to think beyond "business as usual" scenarios, or who are beholden to a single view of the future may put the scenario planning project at risk. These people are helpful on the outside of the project, because their potential critique will prompt the development of rigorous scenarios; however, having them on the team carries much potential to derail the team from keeping to the method. Aim to have at least a few creative thinkers involved who are known to challenge assumptions and come up with interesting ideas.

Who will facilitate the method?

Most scenario planning projects benefit from being facilitated by someone who understands scenario planning, who has experience with scenario planning methods (not necessarily with climate change), and who doesn't have any conflicts of interest surrounding the project. The facilitator plays a key role in keeping the team and the organization moving forward through the method. This person may be someone inside the organization (which may help to keep your costs down), or an external consultant (which may provide someone who is seen as neutral), but needs to be someone who is acceptable to the CEO, President, and project champion. Ralston and Wilson added that the facilitator needs "an ability to stimulate open-mindedness and a reach beyond conventional thinking on the part of the scenario team."[6]

Once you have identified a champion and gained support from leadership, appointed a team leader and possibly a facilitator, and have assembled your team, you are ready to convene the first workshop. See Box 2.1 for suggestions about your first workshop.

BOX 2.1 INITIAL WORKSHOP

Once all the above people are in place, convene a workshop of 1–2 days to give the project a formal beginning. Consider providing each team member with a copy of this book so they have it as a reference, and ask them to read it before the workshop. In consultation with any facilitator, consider including the following elements:

- **Opening:** Have the project champion, the CEO, or similar senior person open the meeting, explain why the project is being undertaken, the aims of the project, the scope of the project, its audience, and highlight their support for it. They can then introduce the project manager, who can (with any facilitator) start the main part of the meeting.
- **Provide an overview of scenario planning,** the scenario planning method the project will follow, and the timeline
- **Provide an overview of climate change,** and facilitate discussion based on questions such as "How have we been affected by climate, climate-related policy, or other climate-related issues in the past, and how did we respond?" and "How might we be affected by climate change issues in future?"

- **Define the focal question**, and discuss its importance. If the project will define its own question, include time to discuss and complete it
- **Define the time horizon**, and explain its significance. If the project will define a time horizon different than 25 years, include time to discuss and complete it
- **Identifying key external stakeholders:** Set a goal of identifying them at the workshop.
- If time permits, begin identifying driving forces (see Chapter 3 for details)
- **Conclusion:** To conclude the workshop, hold a plenary session that summarizes what has been achieved so far - focal question, time horizon, list of external stakeholders, and possibly an initial list of potential driving forces – and outline next steps and any deadlines.

Define the focal question

The focal question is the anchor for many of the decisions made while following the method. Most importantly, the nature of the focal question will determine how you carry out the method. As Kees van der Heijden[4] noted in his book, *Scenarios: The Art of Strategic Conversation*, your team can use an inductive or deductive approach to scenario planning. Other approaches have been developed, which Ramírez and Wilkinson[14] review, most of which are grounded in deduction, induction, or a combination of the two. It's important to understand the difference between them so you can start out on the right track.

Your focal question needs to be worded in a way that supports your inductive or deductive approach. If you approach scenario planning using inductive reasoning, then you will set a focal question with an open-ended outcome, and identify drivers to develop scenarios that explore those potential outcomes. Inductive scenario planning questions broadly ask "What combinations of drivers seem important, what outcome scenarios could plausibly develop from them, what should we do, and when?"

Alternately, if you take a deductive approach to scenario planning, then you will propose (or set) a potential outcome, and work backwards from it to identify drivers and develop scenarios that could plausibly lead to that outcome. Deductive questions broadly ask "What combinations of drivers could plausibly lead to a specific (often bad) outcome scenario, what should we do, and when?" Examples of the specified outcome scenario may include operations being closed temporarily or permanently (or for that matter flourishing) unexpectedly due to climate-related phenomena. This will help you develop strategic options to prepare for that situation. The latter deductive option may seem extreme, but Entergy New Orleans (ENO) probably wished it had considered such a question before it was hit by Hurricane Katrina:

> *Hurricane Katrina not only caused catastrophic and unprecedented damage to ENO's electric and gas facilities, but it also resulted in the loss of most of ENO's customers, an unprecedented occurrence in the U.S. Utility Industry.*[15: 1]

The dual impact of damaged infrastructure and loss of its consumer market was catastrophic, and although ENO did not mention how its suppliers were affected, Department of Energy[15] records dated December 5, 2005 (more than three months after Katrina made landfall) reported that, "34% of Gulf Coast oil production, 27% of gas production and some of the largest refineries remained shut."[16]

As you can see, the deductive methods have a particular outcome in mind, while inductive methods do not. I have suggested a broad inductive question in this book that I will follow as the method progresses, but the method will help you with either inductive or deductive approaches to scenario planning for climate change. The key thing to remember when choosing an inductive or deductive question is that it needs to help you focus on the uncertainty for which you want to prepare.

The sample question this book will follow, is **"How could climate change plausibly affect our organization, what should we do, and when?"** This question allows the scenario planning team to look for evidence pointing to particular climate drivers, and develop plausible outcome scenarios from those drivers. Here is a deductive version of the question (you might choose between closing, flourishing, or status quo outcome, or a larger project could examine all three): "What climate change events could plausibly lead to our organization to temporarily or permanently close/flourish unexpectedly, or the status quo continuing, what should we do, and when?" Notice that both versions of the question have three parts: 1) "How could climate change plausibly affect our organization?" or "What climate change events could plausibly lead to our organization to temporarily or permanently close/flourish unexpectedly, or the status quo continuing"; 2) "What should we do?"; and 3) "When?" While you could focus only on the first part if resources, time, or organizational politics deem it necessary, this book will help you to answer all parts so you can understand the potential outcomes and what could lead to them, develop strategies in response to them, and decide at what point they should be implemented.

The sample question has the organization as the level of analysis; however, it's not uncommon to develop a question for a specific part of an organization rather than a whole organization. For instance, "How could climate change plausibly affect our South Carolina production plant, what should we do, and when?", or "How could climate change plausibly affect our service unit, what should we do, and when?", or even "How could climate change plausibly affect our beverage products, what should we do, and when?" As Mats Lindgren and Hans Bandhold[17] mention in their book *Scenario Planning: The Link Between Future and Strategy*, even if you start the project with a focus on the broader organization-wide level, once you get started it may become necessary to look more closely at a specific part of it.

If you are considering developing a different question than the sample question, or a sub-organizational level of analysis, below are a few primer questions to consider, and examples of inductive and deductive questions. As you will see, the scenario planning question (and the method) is scalable and can be applied to an aspect of an organization, or the whole organization. These questions will help you establish the scope of your question, and decide whether it would be better examined inductively or deductively:

- On what external forces does the organization's business model primarily depend? That is, what affects the ability to create value for customers, charge a certain price for that value, and the costs involved in creating that value?

  a   Example inductive question: How could climate change plausibly affect our business model, what should we do, and when?

  b   Example deductive question: What climate change events could plausibly lead to our business model to collapse/flourish unexpectedly, or the status quo continuing, what should we do, and when?

- What is the most mission critical part of the organization? Examples might include a particular asset, process, resource, geographic location, or group.

  a   Example inductive question: How could climate change events plausibly affect [mission critical part], what should we do, and when?

  b   Example deductive question: What climate change events could plausibly lead to [mission critical part] temporarily or permanently closing/flourishing unexpectedly, or the status quo continuing, what should we do, and when?

- Which product, process, market, location or asset contains the most investment in terms of time, effort and money? On what does its sustainability depend?

  a   Example inductive question: How could climate change plausibly affect the [product/process/market/location/asset], what should we do, and when?

  b   Example deductive question: What climate change events could plausibly lead to [product/process/market/location/asset] temporarily or permanently closing/flourishing unexpectedly, or the status quo continuing, what should we do, and when?

- Is there a current strategy or project that will greatly influence the future of the organization? Examples might include expanding into a new market, a significant acquisition, investing in a new technology, or developing a new product range. What determines the success of that strategy or project?

  a   Example inductive question: How could climate change events plausibly affect the strategy, what should we do, and when?

  b   Example deductive question: What climate change events could plausibly lead the organization to [abandon the strategy at significant sunk cost/ invest more in the strategy at significant opportunity cost/continue with the strategy as planned], what should we do, and when?

In the above questions I have also borrowed Peter Schwartz's[10] idea of approaching the question from optimistic, pessimistic, and status quo views so your dominant view will become visible. If as you work through the questions above you find yourself questioning or dismissing negative possibilities then you may be experiencing optimism bias. If, on the other hand you find yourself questioning or dismissing positive possibilities, you may be more of a pessimist. Considering what will be required to bring the status quo into being may also help you see how implausible it is over the medium and long term given that nothing remains constant. Your view may change over time, and you may find yourself being more pessimistic or optimistic in relation to some aspects, and lean towards the status quo in others. Similarly, you may have positive, neutral, or negative attitudes about particular actors and institutions surrounding the questions for a variety of reasons. It is important to note all these reactions because it helps to bring your assumptions and biases to the surface so you can acknowledge them and develop a clearer understanding.

It will be evident by now that the nature of discussions when developing the question make it imperative that key decision-makers are in the main scenario planning team and are in attendance. Since they will likely be the key audience for your scenarios, their knowledge about the organization, its operations and its strategic landscape will help to make the question (thus the scenarios) relevant.

Define the time horizon

The question will really start to come to life once it is put into the context of a time horizon (or "horizon date"[18]), because the time horizon prescribes the year in which the scenarios will be set, and this influences research plans to identify and analyze the driving forces.[1] The time horizon needs to be meaningful for the level of analysis (the organization, business unit, or location), the context of the focal question (here, climate change), and to the audience (organizational decision-makers).

It is important to arrive at a time horizon that strikes a balance between not being so long as to produce vague scenarios to which nobody can relate, and not being so short as to produce scenarios that require little research and do nothing to prepare the organization for surprises. In their book *The Mind of a Fox: Scenario Planning in Action*, Chantell Ilbury and Clem Sunter called this phenomenon a "cone of uncertainty":[19] The further out your time horizon is, the more uncertainty there is about the nature of any given scenario. This uncertainty needs to be balanced with the aim of preparing the organization for the long term.

In workshops and classes where I teach scenario planning, I introduce people to scenario planning by taking them through a condensed 90-minute scenario planning exercise based on the question "How could my career look 15 years from now, and how should I prepare?" If there are people in the room who are planning to retire by that time, they consider the question "How could my retirement look 15 years from now and how should I prepare?" A career or retirement is something most people will readily relate to and have thought a lot about, so they will know enough about it to make it a useful exercise based on their existing knowledge without doing too much additional research in the moment. The time horizon is long enough that it requires people to do a little research to examine the potential relevance of their skills, technology developments in their field, the state of retirement accounts, their health, real estate investments, etc., but short enough to produce useful scenarios.

Leading people through this condensed scenario planning project puts them through the surprises and challenges presented by the method on a topic that is important to them, and importantly, underscores the need for a meaningful time horizon.

In this book, I use 25 years as a scenario planning time horizon, which in my experience strikes a balance between challenging organizational thinking beyond a five-year strategic plan and out to the life of a long-term investment, and is just long enough for the current state of climate science to support good research and scenarios. However, if 25 years is not as useful to your organization, consider the following questions, which will help you determine the most appropriate time horizon for your scenario planning project:

- The organization:

    a   What is the organization's longest-term investment or asset? Perhaps it is a capital asset like a building, a piece of land, or perhaps a shareholding, or accounts for contractual benefits such as retirement and/or health benefits.

    b   What is the organization's longest-term financing or funding agreement? Mortgages or other loans, credit arrangements, venture capital agreements, philanthropic or grant funding, and other such arrangements all fall into this category.

    c   What other long-term contractual agreements has the organization entered? For instance, does it have any long-term leases, rental agreements, partnerships, options, employee benefit contracts, or customer or supply contracts?

    d   What is the organization's longest-term plan or strategy? This may be the strategic plan, a product development lifecycle, or any other plan.

- The strategic environment. Answering these questions may require a little reading ahead and research, but also may affect the choice of time horizon (the final three questions are prompted by Paul Schoemaker's overview of scenario planning published in the *Sloan Management Review*[12]):

    a   Which climate drivers might affect the organization and at what point in time?

    b   How often do large shifts occur in the expectations of your customers?

    c   How often do large shifts occur in the regulation of your field or industry?

    d   How often do major technologies change in your field or industry?

    e   How long are your competitors' time horizons?

    f   How long is the political election cycle?

Finally, if time and resources permit, you could even consider running parallel scenario analyses using various time horizons.

Identify key external stakeholders

Professor Edward Freeman at the University of Virginia defined stakeholders as "... any group or individual who can affect or is affected by the achievement of the organization's objectives."[20: 46] As Freeman's definition suggests, any organization likely has many stakeholders that affect or are affected by it, its products, its investment decisions, etc. In this step, you will identify your key stakeholders in general, but especially those that are important to your focal question. The purpose of identifying your key external stakeholders now is three-fold:

1. You may identify additional key stakeholders (e.g. important suppliers or customers) that you may want to have some role on the scenario planning project;
2. As you identify potential driving forces, you might find that uncertainties emerge from your key stakeholders. In its study of business resilience and climate change, the Center for Climate and Energy Solutions found that even though many large companies had "extensive internal resources" from which to draw in the face of climate change issues, their suppliers often did not, which left these companies exposed to climate risks. Some of their interviewees stated that "there was also limited communication with suppliers on the issue of climate vulnerability",[21] which increases the risk. Infrastructure providers and city planners are also key stakeholders, and organizations can similarly be at risk if the infrastructure on which they rely is left exposed. These issues led the Center for Climate and Energy Solutions to conclude that "critical supply chains and infrastructure... can be effectively managed only in partnership with the public sector."[21] Two-thirds of cities around the world are already collaborating with businesses on reducing their carbon emissions and adapting to the physical impacts of climate change, and over 50% are engaging the private sector in climate projects.[22] It would be prudent to consider how your organization might learn from these kinds of stakeholders.
3. It is useful to identify key stakeholders and their positions, incentives and motivations towards climate change now, so that once you develop your scenarios, you can anticipate how they might respond, and how their responses might affect your organization's development of strategic options.

A starting list of potential stakeholders might include many of those on the following list. Add to or subtract from the list, and identify which might be important to your organization by working through each item, asking: Is this potential stakeholder important for the organization in relation to climate change, and if so why? Asking this question will help you to identify which stakeholders are potentially important in relation to your focal question.

- Board members
- Customers
- Suppliers

- Employees
- Unions
- Shareholders and other types of investors
- Social media followers
- Financiers and creditors
- Insurers
- Benefactors and patrons
- Beneficiaries
- Community members and organizers
- Community and neighborhood associations
- Industry or business associations, or chambers of commerce
- Policymakers and regulators
- Local utilities and infrastructure providers (energy, water, transportation, communications)
- Co-located organizations
- Long-term lessors
- Town planners
- Civil defense organizations and managers of local emergency responses
- Users
- News media

Adding further to the list, Schoemaker[12] also noted that "in the environmental area, judges, scientists, lawyers" are becoming more powerful as stakeholders. As you work through the list, you may need to think ahead a little to consider how your organization and any particular stakeholder might be affected by climate change, but you can continue to edit your list of stakeholders as you continue to work through the method.

At this point, you have the basics of your scenario planning project: A champion, a project manager, potentially a facilitator, a team representing various parts of the organization, a focal question, a time horizon, and you've identified key external stakeholders. If any senior executives involved in the project have not been fully engaged up to this point, now is an excellent time to meet with them to give them a detailed debriefing of the progress thus far, before moving on to Step 2.

Note

1 If you want to dive more deeply into the social and cultural aspects of time as they relate to scenario planning, Ramírez and Wilkinson provide a good overview in their book *Strategic Reframing: The Oxford Scenario Planning Approach*.

References

1 Shell. 2008. *Scenarios: An Explorer's Guide. Exploring the Future*. The Hague: Shell International BV.

2 TCFD. 2016. *The Use of Scenario Analysis in Disclosure of Climate-Related Risks and Opportunities*. Financial Stability Board Task Force on Climate-Related Financial Disclosures. https://www.fsb-tcfd.org/publications/technical-supplement/#, accessed 20 Feb 2017.

3 Chermack, T.J. 2011. *Scenario Planning in Organizations: How to Create, Use, and Assess Scenarios*. Oakland, CA: Berrett-Koehler.

4 van der Heijden, K. 2005. *Scenarios: The Art of Strategic Conversation*. 2nd edn. Chichester, UK: John Wiley & Sons.

5 Kahane, A. 2012. *Transformative Scenario Planning: Working Together to Change the Future*. San Francisco: Berrett-Koehler.

6 Ralston, B. and I. Wilson. 2006. *The Scenario-Planning Handbook: A Practitioner's Guide to Developing and Using Scenarios to Direct Strategy in Today's Uncertain Times*. Mason, OH: Thomson/South-Western.

7 Randall, R.M. and L. Fahey. 1998. Integrating strategy and scenarios, in *Learning from the Future: Competitive Foresight Scenarios*, ed. L. Fahey and R.M. Randall. New York: John Wiley & Sons. pp. 22–38.

8 Schoemaker, P.J.H. 1998. Twenty common pitfalls in scenario planning, in *Learning from the Future: Competitive Foresight Scenarios*, ed. L. Fahey and R.M. Randall. New York: John Wiley & Sons. pp. 422–431.

9 Wack, P. 1985. Scenarios: Shooting the rapids, *Harvard Business Review*, 63/6: 139–150.

10 Schwartz, P. 1996. *The Art of the Long View: Planning for the Future in an Uncertain World*. New York: Doubleday.

11 Elahi, S. and R. Ramírez. 2016. European Patent Office case study, in *Strategic Reframing: The Oxford Scenario Planning Approach*, ed. R. Ramírez and A. Wilkinson. Oxford: Oxford University Press. pp. 201–207.

12 Schoemaker, P.J.H. 1995. Scenario planning: A tool for strategic thinking, *Sloan Management Review*, 36/2: 25–40.

13 Wade, W. 2012. *Scenario Planning: A Field Guide to the Future*. Hoboken, USA: John Wiley & Sons.

14 Ramírez, R. and A. Wilkinson. 2016. *Strategic Reframing: The Oxford Scenario Planning Approach*. Oxford: Oxford University Press.

15 DOE. 2005. *Gulf Coast hurricanes situation report #44*. US Department of Energy.

16 Haigh, N.L. and A. Griffiths. 2009. The natural environment as primary stakeholder: The case of climate change, *Business Strategy and the Environment*, 18/6: 347–359.

17 Lindgren, M. and H. Bandhold. 2009. *Scenario Planning: The Link Between Future and Strategy*. 2nd edn. Houndmills, UK: Palgrave Macmillan.

18 Wilkinson, A. and R. Kupers. 2013. Living in the futures, *Harvard Business Review*, 91/5: 118–127.

19 Ilbury, C. and C. Sunter. 2001. *The Mind of a Fox: Scenario Planning in Action*. Cape Town: Human & Rousseau/Tafelberg Publishers.

20 Freeman, R.E. 1984. *Strategic Management: A Stakeholder Approach*. Business and Public Policy, ed. E.M. Epstein. Boston: Pitman.

21 C2ES. 2015. *Weathering the Next Storm: A Closer Look at Business Resilience*. Center for Climate and Energy Solutions.

22 CDP. 2016. It takes a city: The case for collaborative climate action. Carbon Disclosure Project. https://b8f65cb373b1b7b15feb-c70d8ead6ced550b4d987d7c03fcdd1d.ssl.cf3.rackcdn.com/cms/reports/documents/000/001/172/original/CDP_Thematic-Report_2016.pdf?1475744852, accessed 18 April 2017.

3

STEP 2: IDENTIFY, SPECIFY, AND RANK THE DRIVING FORCES

Good scenarios depend on your ability to identify the underlying driving forces that could shape your organization's future in relation to the focal question, and to rank them to determine which will be used to develop plausible, relevant scenarios. This step will guide you through identifying the forces that are, in combination, most uncertain and potentially most impactful for your organization, and that could go in various directions to affect the organization's future. The outcome of this step is a ranked list of drivers from which you will build your scenarios.

Activities within this step are typically the most time and energy intensive because they require a great deal of research. Some of the research will involve broad-based inquiries to identify the driving forces that may affect your organization (the Appendix can help you start this). For each identified driving force you will then need to conduct specific inquiries to determine past trends and events, and possible future states, and the potential ways it can affect your organization and its key stakeholders. Something else that adds to the time involved in this step is the iteration it can involve, as you shift from broad-based identification of driving forces into specifying them in detail, and then potentially back out if you decide that what you first thought was a driving force is really an outcome of another driving force, or vice versa. I have seen people get themselves into conceptual puzzles as they iterate between identifying, specifying, and ranking forces, so while I have set the method out linearly below, expect some iteration to occur. The research for and specifying of drivers needs to be complete before you can effectively rank them and move to the next step of building scenarios.

It is important to conduct detailed research and not to skip it, cut corners, or otherwise short-circuit this step, because insights you gain will help you to create scenarios that are full of nuanced, rich, real-world, plausible details. Without detailed research, your scenarios will be significantly less effective, and probably useless, for strategy development. Your research may take you several layers deep into unfamiliar, unconventional, surprising, and maybe even peculiar sub-topics that are way outside your realm of expertise and potentially outside your comfort zone – this is completely normal.

It is also important to keep the scope of work in this step reined in so it remains manageable and does not expand the overall scope of the project. The project leader will need to keep a keen eye on scope creep during this step, and make strong calls about what is relevant and in scope vs. what emergent knowledge needs to remain out of scope. One good tool I've used to rein in the scope of projects (or even meetings) is the "parking lot." Any insights, knowledge, data, or points of view that do not appear directly relevant to the focal question or cannot be extrapolated or interpolated to the time horizon are recorded in a separate document (or separate PowerPoint slide) called the parking lot, along with the name of the contributor. Additions to the parking lot are revisited later if needed. The power of the parking lot is that it ensures everyone's contributions are recorded, while keeping things moving forward with what is currently in scope. I usually revisit the parking lot when needed or at the next meeting, and items are addressed if needed, kept in the parking lot for later, or removed if they are no longer deemed relevant. In my experience, many parking lot items simply fade away with time, while a few will filter into the project at later stages.

A benefit of using the method laid out in this book is that it will help you to maintain transparency in your scenario planning process, which is valuable for helping others to understand how driving forces are identified. This is important for others wanting to replicate the method in future. As the TCFD noted:

> Transparency around key parameters, assumptions, and analytical choices will help to support comparability of results between different scenarios used by an organization and across organizations. In turn, this will support the evaluation, by analysts and investors, of the potential magnitude and timing of impacts on individual organizations and sectors and the robustness of organizations' strategies across the range of plausible impacts, thereby supporting better risk and capital allocation decisions.[1]

In addition to producing a ranked list of drivers, other useful outcomes from this step include summaries and short presentations of each driving force that include its name, a description, possible state/s of the driver at the time horizon, other forces it may relate to, and how the force may affect the organization. Each sub-step of the method is detailed below.

You may start to identify decisions that would be needed on the basis of a single driver, and feel a strong urge to start strategizing immediately. Rather than strategize now, note your thoughts down so can revisit them in Step 4, when you will be able to strategize with the support of a bigger picture that includes all the drivers and scenarios, rather strategizing based on insights about a single driving force.

Identify driving forces

Your aim is to identify a shortlist of climate change driving forces so you can rank them. Driving forces are those forces that are external to your organization and relevant to your focal question. Identify as many as you can, but take Wilkinson and Kupers'[2] and Schoemaker's[3] advice and don't pressure yourself or your team to try to identify every single possible driving force, because the world is too unpredictable and it's impossible.

To identify driving forces, you will be looking from outside the organization in, rather than from inside the organization out. Unless your organization is very large and politically powerful, it will likely have little to no control over driving forces, because they emerge from a broader macro level. For instance, technological innovation going on inside the organization is not a driving force; rather, it is likely a response to society wanting technologically advanced goods or services, and competition for that business. Even if your organization is very large and politically powerful, and is a broad global driver of technological innovation, it will still have no control over climate change.

A good framework to help scenario planners identify a range of driving forces is the STEEP framework. The STEEP framework is a standard strategic management framework for identifying forces in the strategic environment that may be categorized as Societal, Technological, Economic, Ecological, or Political/Legal. The STEEP framework, or some variation of it, is included in most strategic management texts. You and your team can work through each category to identify potential drivers. The MBA Boost[4] website gives good definitions of each element:

- Social: "The social element of the external environment takes into account the aspects that describe society as a whole. Some of the key elements that organizations must deal with in each market are:

  a   Demographics
  b   Lifestyles
  c   Religion
  d   Education
  e   Age distribution of the population"

- Technological: "[C]hanges within the technological environment [that could affect] product-development strategies."
- Economic: "The economic environment contains aspects dealing with individuals' capacity to obtain products or services given the set of economic conditions."
- Ecological: "The ecological element considers the present-day situation of the physical and biological environments that companies can face."
- Political/Legal: "[t]he political and legal environments of a specific country or region where companies select to operate."

The driving forces you identify may affect the organization directly, or may affect one or more of its key stakeholders and therefore affect the organization indirectly (but still significantly). They may also bring potential positive or negative impacts; though in my experience most climate change driving forces bring more threats than opportunities.

Some climate change driving forces will be known and obvious to you based on previous experience. For instance, if the organization's critical assets are located on low-lying coastal land in a hurricane-prone area, and they have been affected by a hurricane before, then you may already be thinking that extreme weather is a likely candidate for being a driving force. However, other potential driving forces may not be as obvious, such as the degree to which an essential production input, or a key supplier, customer, or competitor is vulnerable to a climate driver, the degree to which local utilities are developing climate resilient infrastructure, or how climate drivers might affect market preferences.

Two things you can do to identify climate change forces are: First, read (and suggest the team reads) the Appendix at the back of the book. Second, hold a workshop with the team to identify and discuss potential drivers. Both of these are covered below.

Review climate drivers

In the back of the book, the Appendix provides you with overviews of some commonly known climate change drivers to help you identify potential drivers relevant to your organization. The overviews cover all areas of the STEEP framework. Further driver summaries are freely available at www.nardiahaigh.com.

The overview of each driver in the Appendix includes a description of it, how it's affecting organizations now, including examples where possible, and how it could affect organizations in future. If you need to investigate any particular driver further, the sources of all information are cited.

Give team members 2–3 weeks to start doing research, reading the Appendix and companion website, IPCC research, and other reports, to identify several potential climate change drivers. Each team member should take notes to justify the relevance of each driver to your organization, and identify potential risks and opportunities each presents. These notes will help everyone contribute to the next workshop to identify drivers.

The importance of maps to climate change scenario planning

Maps are a key visual element to help you identify and analyze climate change drivers, because they will help you define the geographic scope of your project. IPCC reports cited throughout this book, and recent ones re-cited here[5, 6, 7] provide many maps depicting the geographic distribution of historical and projected trends in physical climate drivers, such as temperature change, precipitation change, extreme weather, snow cover, and ocean temperature. IPCC maps are key to my own scenario planning workshops, because most people can easily take in visual information. Consult with IPCC maps, and on them plot the geographic locations of your organization's assets and operations, key suppliers and production inputs, and key customers and broader markets, so you can make notes about potential impacts as your research progresses. You might also consider obtaining maps of water, energy, communications, and health infrastructure surrounding capital assets and operations. Provide these maps to all team members.

As you identify each driving force, write it down to begin a list of broad drivers. In Table 3.1 I have written the names of several example drivers on a ranking spreadsheet developed to help you rank them. The spreadsheet is available for you to download at www.nardiahaigh.com or you can easily develop your own.

Table 3.1 is the first part of a progressive example for a hypothetical local bank based in Boston I call LocalBank, Inc. The hypothetical LocalBank is based on an amalgamation of scenario planning reports done by executives and students in my classes focused on urban banks in various U.S. cities. I base LocalBank in Boston, because I understand its climate vulnerabilities. Assume LocalBank is a publicly listed savings bank serving local Boston communities, is a commercial and personal lender, and has branches all around Boston. LocalBank has hypothetical assets worth approximately $3 billion, around $2.4 billion in customer loans, and $2.05 billion in customer deposits. LocalBank's loan portfolio includes personal loans, short-term commercial loans, construction loans, mortgages, commercial and industrial loans, and commercial real estate loans. Its deposits include individual and business checking and savings accounts, and small and large term deposits. LocalBank is profitable, has been growing and has aspirations for further growth through acquisition and organic growth, and is investing in this direction. Table 3.1 contains an example list of initial driving forces you might identify for LocalBank. Your own list may have many more, or fewer. Note that while I've included the rating and ranking columns in the spreadsheet, you can ignore them until we get to those steps.

Identify and discuss driving forces

Once each team member has a list of several potential climate change drivers, like that in Table 3.1, bring everyone together in a workshop to identify a broad list of potential climate change drivers. Refer to Box 3.1 for suggestions about the content and structure of the workshop.

TABLE 3.1 Initial list of potential climate change drivers for LocalBank

Ranking the driving forces			
Driving force	A. Uncertainty rating	B. Impact rating	Total (A×B)
Increased intensity and frequency of extreme weather events			
Sea level rise			
Increased efforts by City to adapt infra-structure to changing climate			
More stringent local and national carbon emissions policies			

BOX 3.1 CLIMATE DRIVER IDENTIFICATION WORKSHOP

Convene a workshop of 1–2 days to identify climate change drivers. Everyone should bring their notes and research materials to the workshop for reference, and be prepared to continue doing research in the workshop in collaboration with other team members. As a structure for the workshop, and in consultation with any facilitator, consider the following elements:

- **Opening:** Open the workshop by stating the aim of identifying climate change drivers. If time and project scope permits, you may be able to achieve more by combining this workshop with the next one to rate and rank the forces; though more preparation for this combined workshop will be required
- **Develop a list of potential drivers:** Develop a broad list of potential drivers from a whole team discussion of everyone's initial research: Focusing on the first part of your focal question, which for the purpose of this book is "How could climate change plausibly affect our organization?" pose a starting list of potential drivers based on previous interviews and discussions, your research, and any relevant forces from the Appendix. Each person suggesting a potential driver should justify how it might affect the organization and cite any sources they found from doing their research. Don't exclude any potential drivers at this point. Have the growing list on a screen so everyone can see it.
- **Assign drivers to individuals/groups for initial research:** Cluster the drivers by type and assign them to break-out groups for a morning or afternoon session in which each group focuses on specifying the scope and level of analysis for each driver, doing further research to determine plausible state/s at the time horizon, and relevant trends and events. Each group should start a document to summarize each driver. These summaries will become key working documents as the method proceeds. The summaries in Appendix A can serve as a template for organization-specific summaries.
- **Individuals/groups report back to team:** Have each break-out group report the results of their further research back to the team, take onboard any immediate feedback, and update the master list of potential climate drivers (example in Table 3.3).
- **Assign potential drivers for further research:** Report the resulting list of potential climate drivers to everyone, and assign responsibility to individuals/groups for undertaking further research to rate the plausible uncertainty and impact of each driver before the next workshop.
- **Conclusion:** Summarize what has been achieved – a list of driving forces for further investigation, or as far as you got in the process, and individuals/groups assigned to rate plausible uncertainty and impacts before next workshop, and the date of the next workshop.

A challenge for this workshop is not only to identify known drivers, but to also consider other potential drivers that may currently be vague, unquantifiable, or ambiguous. Including these less-identifiable drivers will help people to avoid assuming the future will replicate the past, and avoid blind spots. You might end up with a list of drivers in a similar fashion to those listed in Table 3.2.

In Table 3.2, note that the initial individual list has been expanded considerably to include a range of other potential drivers. Temperature change has also been broken out into land and ocean temperature change, and notes have been added about potential trends and other drivers to which they relate.

Having the right mix of people involved in the team will bear fruit at this point, because each person will bring different insights about the drivers based on their own expertise, experience, and research. After the break-out groups you could end up with a more detailed list of potential drivers, such as that for LocalBank in Table 3.3.

TABLE 3.2 Initial workshop list of potential climate change drivers for LocalBank

Ranking the driving forces

Driving force	A. Uncertainty rating	B. Impact rating	Total (A×B)
Extreme weather events: Increased intensity and frequency of storms			
Sea level change: Rising sea levels and storm surge			
Infrastructure adaptation: Increased action by City and State to adapt infra-structure and landscape to climate change (relates to sea level rise, extreme weather)			
Carbon emissions policies: More stringent local and national policies			
Precipitation: More rain and less snow (relates to temperature rise)			
Human migration: People moving away from hazardous areas (relates to extreme weather, sea level rise, damage to coastal properties)			
Ambient temperature over land: Rising temperature over land			
Ocean temperature: Rising ocean temperature			
Snow cover: Reduced snow cover in winter (relates to precipitation and temperature)			
Damage to coastal properties: From river/coastal/urban flooding (relates to sea level rise, extreme weather, infrastructure adaptation)			

TABLE 3.3 Final workshop list of potential climate change drivers for LocalBank

Ranking the driving forces

Driving force	A. Uncertainty rating	B. Impact rating	Total (A×B)
Extreme weather events: By [year of 25-year time horizon], extreme weather will increase in intensity and incidence, significantly affecting operations and collateral properties every 3–4 years.			
Sea level change: By [year of 25-year time horizon], sea levels will rise by 12″ in Boston, causing regular flooding at high tide, and exacerbating storm surge damage. (relates to extreme weather)			
Infrastructure adaptation: By [year of 25-year time horizon], there will be significant efforts by City and State to adapt infrastructure and landscape to changing climate. (relates to sea level rise, extreme weather)			
Carbon emissions policies: By [year of 25-year time horizon], national policies to curb carbon emissions will be in place, and State policies will be more stringent.			
Precipitation: By [year of 25-year time horizon], more precipitation will fall as rain and less as snow. (relates to temperature rise)			
Human migration: By [year of 25-year time horizon], people will be moving away from hazardous areas to live in safer areas. (relates to extreme weather, sea level rise, damage to coastal properties)			
Ambient temperature over land: By [year of 25-year time horizon], land temperature will rise by 1.5°F and Boston will experience more heatwaves.			
Ocean temperature: By [year of 25-year time horizon], ocean temperature will rise by 2°F, keeping Atlantic hurricanes alive as they progress up the coast to Massachusetts. (relates to extreme weather)			
Snow cover: By [year of 25-year time horizon], there will be less snow cover in winter. (relates to precipitation and temperature)			
Damage to coastal properties: By [year of 25-year time horizon], property damage from river/coastal/urban flooding will increase significantly in incidence and severity. (relates to sea level rise, extreme weather, infrastructure adaptation)			

In Table 3.3, further details of each potential driver are added, including the time horizon, and any specific plausible projections that can be found. The figures I have added for temperature and sea level change are loosely interpolated from 2014 IPCC reports, but you should do your own digging into the latest research rather than rely on them. They are purely for the purposes of the hypothetical example. Also note that the forces are written in definite terms, like "more precipitation *will* fall" rather than "more precipitation *may* fall" – since you will examine the uncertainty in the next step you should not write it into your driver descriptions as well. If you try to manage the uncertainty when describing the force in the spreadsheet your research and scenarios will become convoluted and less meaningful. Also note that at this point the potential drivers are not very specific in terms of their scope and level of analysis, so several of them will be removed or combined soon.

Towards the end of this workshop, assign specific people or teams responsibility for further post-workshop research about each driver, or group of drivers, with the aim of fleshing out the details of each driver, and determining plausible uncertainty and impact ratings. This work needs to be done prior to the next workshop where the drivers will be rated and ranked. These people or teams may be based on any break-out groups you formed, and they should assume ownership of the climate summaries for their specific drivers, because they will develop them further.

Below are a few notes on defining and specifying the scope and level of analysis for each driving force, which will help lay the groundwork for rating uncertainty and impact.

Define each driving force

As you think about each potential driving force, it will be useful if you can accurately label and to some degree define it. Peter Schwartz warns about treating definitions too rigidly.[8] I'm not suggesting that you be rigid with your definitions, but a good label and broad definition can help to reduce the ambiguity for first-time scenario planners. Find a scientific or generally accepted label and definition for each, and include them in the climate driver summary and any draft project report you are developing. If you are able to adopt the label and terminology of a known definition, it will ensure you are discussing it using the same vocabulary as everyone else around the world doing the same thing, and this will help you when you need to communicate with experts, policymakers, town planners, and others.

Specify each driving force

It's important to specify the most appropriate scope and level of analysis for your driving forces, so your research can remain focused. The key is to identify a scope that is not too large or small, and a level of analysis that is not too distant or too close. This will help you avoid scenarios that are too vague or too myopic, and help you avoid becoming overwhelmed with the research. Paralysis by analysis is easy to experience when doing scenario planning research, so keeping it to a minimum is crucial.

Specifying the scope is important and relatively easy, since you already decided whether you are conducting your scenario planning project for the whole organization, or a specific asset, market, region, etc., but the scope of the driver may be a little different, because you will want to specify the scope of *impact*. Would the driver affect neighbors, suppliers, customers, or directly impact the organization? As you investigate each driver, you may find that the geographic scope of the project expands. For instance, the hypothetical LocalBank might initially focus on how the drivers in Table 3.3 could affect the locations of its Boston branches, then look closely at its loan portfolio to see that properties in low-lying coastal areas or areas prone to inland flooding north, south, east and west of Boston are being used as collateral for loans, and thus present a broader geographic area than first thought.

Specifying the level of analysis is also important, and can be conceptually more complex, because part of this specification is determining whether it is useful to consider something as a driver in its own right, or as a part or outcome of another higher-level driver. On one hand, you might argue that rising concentrations of atmospheric greenhouse gases, caused by a mix of human and natural phenomena, influences all drivers, and therefore is the primary driver of other climate change drivers. Scientific research would support your argument, and the concentration of atmospheric greenhouse gases is a good metric to track on a global level. However, forces that are at a conceptually lower level of analysis will be more useful for your analytical purposes, such as sea level rise and policy change, because at these levels you can begin to discuss potential organizational uncertainties and impacts relating to new regulation or flooding, which is more useful for developing scenarios and strategies. On the other hand, if you have identified many granular driving forces, some of which are the outcomes of higher-level forces, it will help to consolidate them under the highest meaningful level of analysis so you can avoid doubling up on your analysis.

For instance, Table 3.3 for LocalBank includes several potential drivers that discussion would determine whether it's better to treat them as drivers in their own right, or as outcomes of higher level drivers. Two potential drivers currently listed are "human migration" and "damage to coastal properties." It may be more useful to think of these drivers as outcomes of the dynamics between sea level rise, infrastructure adaptation, and extreme weather, so one might remove them from the list during the specification process, and they would be noted as a potential impacts of those other forces. Similarly, it might be more useful to think about the "snow cover" potential driver as an outcome of changing precipitation, so these two might be combined. Further, you could think about "infrastructure adaptation" as an outcome of sea level rise and extreme weather, but since City and State governments are involved, and the organization has no control over them, it may be better to leave this as a driver in its own right.

Specifying the driving forces is an iterative process that can take you through conceptual twists and turns. If you feel yourself getting to a point of paralysis by analysis (or just feeling frustrated or overwhelmed), take a conceptual step back up to the main driver to reduce the number of sub-topics in play until you get comfortable with that level, remind yourself of the focal question, and then return to take what information you need from sub-topics. Remember that your decision to focus on a particular driver and information from any given sub-topic is completely reversible. Identifying, specifying, and ranking the drivers will likely include some iteration between broad research and sub-topic research to see if they are relevant (and if so, how), then applying this information back to the broader driver and your focal question. If you get to a point of thinking you need to do a whole scenario planning project for a particular driver (now, before you develop the main scenarios), you may be in too deep and need to pull back a little, and you may have multiple drivers encapsulated within this driver that would be better separated.

As you specify your driving forces, update your spreadsheet entries to contain more detail, and show any deletions and amalgamations of forces. Taking onboard several deletions and combinations, Table 3.4 shows a next-step table for LocalBank.

Undertake further research

For every driving force identified, you will need to review scientific research, review information available online, talk to stakeholders and experts inside and outside the organization so you can examine the nature of the force, whether it's relevant to your project, how it is trending (historical trends and projections), whether there are any potential breaks or tipping points in its trend, events that may occur, and what the state of it might be at your time horizon. Below are a few tips to help this research progress.

Read widely

Getting back to the earlier point of not becoming overwhelmed in your research, start by reading, watching, and listening broadly about each force and you will soon get to a point of identifying key sources that you will refer back to and therefore should keep in your records. Be discerning in your research and look for evidence from reputable sources, preferably scientific evidence for which you are able to locate the original source, rather than taking the word of secondary sources. For example, Wikipedia is a good source for gaining a general overview of a force, but since anyone can edit the online encyclopedia its content needs to be viewed with critical eyes, and you should go to the cited sources at the bottom of each Wiki page to verify all claims made. Follow those citations to the original source and read the original claims for yourself – you might be surprised about how much original work is mis-quoted, used out of context, or is spun to support someone's particular political agenda. Similarly, your online research results might yield news media pages (newspapers, magazines, etc.), YouTube videos, blogs, social media pages, etc. – these are a fine start, and you should look at the research they cite so you can get the information from the original source, so you are not being misled by fake news or internet trolls. Use databases available to your local library, or if you are or know someone affiliated with a college library or other organizations

TABLE 3.4 Specified list of climate change drivers for LocalBank

Ranking the driving forces

Driving force	*A. Uncertainty rating*	*B. Impact rating*	Total (A×B)
Extreme weather events: By [year of 25-year time horizon], extreme weather will increase in intensity and incidence, significantly affecting operations, and causing collateral property damage and people to move away every 3–4 years.			
Sea level change: By [year of 25-year time horizon], sea levels will rise by 12″ in Boston, causing regular flooding at high tide, and exacerbating storm surge damage and property damage, causing people to move away. (relates to extreme weather)			
Infrastructure adaptation: By [year of 25-year time horizon], there will be significant efforts by City and State to adapt infrastructure and landscape to changing climate that will reduce property damage and human migration. (relates to sea level rise, extreme weather)			
Carbon emissions policies: By [year of 25-year time horizon], national policies to curb carbon emissions will be in place, and State policies will be more stringent.			
Precipitation: By [year of 25-year time horizon], more precipitation will fall as rain and less as snow, leading to less snow cover. (relates to temperature rise)			
Ambient temperature over land: By [year of 25-year time horizon], land temperature will rise by 1.5°F and Boston will experience more heatwaves.			
Ocean temperature: By [year of 25-year time horizon], ocean temperature will rise by 2°F, keeping Atlantic hurricanes alive as they progress up the coast to Massachusetts. (relates to extreme weather)			

that subscribe to scientific databases, then you may also have access to the latest scientific research. As you do your research, be your own devil's advocate – or find someone who will play that role – and look both for evidence that supports and refutes the possibilities for each driving force. If you are working in a team, everyone can play this role.

Scenario planning also calls you to think about discontinuities that may emerge and have implications for your organization. Consider for example, that incremental temperature increases can cause dramatic tipping points in the supply of water. This occurred in Spring of 2016 at the Kaskawulsh Glacier in Canada's Yukon Territory. A tipping point is a point at which smaller combined changes cause a significant, perhaps sudden and irreversible change. Water from the Kaskawulsh glacier historically flowed into both the Slims River and the Alsek River. The Slims River flows north into the Kluane and then Yukon rivers, where meltwater took a long and winding course eventually into the Bering Sea. By comparison, the Alsek River carries meltwater south over a much shorter course down into the Alaska Gulf. The spring melt of 2016 was particularly strong and the rate of Kaskawulsh Glacier's retreat accelerated, so its meltwater stopped flowing to both rivers, and instead flowed predominantly into the Alsek. Water levels dropped dramatically in the Slims River and Kluane Lake, and rose dramatically in the Alsek. Correspondingly, fish and wildlife populations are being redistributed, water composition altered, and members of small communities that rely on water from the Slims River and Kluane Lake are now further from shore (as is their water infrastructure). The event, which is referred to as "river piracy" was recorded by Daniel Shugar and his colleagues[9] in *Nature Geoscience*, who concluded that "this instance of river piracy was due to post-industrial climate change." Are there possible tipping points in the driving forces you have identified that could affect your organization? Other examples could include disruptive technological developments (e.g. social media, online television and music, smart phones), rapid changes in the political system or an administration (e.g. Brexit, the Arab Spring), extreme weather events (e.g. Super Storm Sandy, flooding from Hurricane Irene), other environmental events (e.g. tsunami, wild fire, severe river flood, sink hole) or tipping points of incremental changes (e.g. drought reaching a point at which water catchments are completely dry, peak electricity demand driven by air-conditioning overwhelming electricity supply infrastructure), economic crises (e.g. the Global Financial Crisis), or sudden shifts in societal sentiment surrounding an issue (e.g. immigrants, asylum seekers, international trade agreements).

Interview experts and thought leaders

Out of your scanning of research and media, you will likely identify people who have expertise on particular drivers, on areas in which the organization's assets are located, on your industry, on climate change, etc. Experts may be industry experts, researchers from universities, research institutes, consulting firms, and others that will provide rigorous information. In addition to using the insights their work provides, you may consider contacting them directly and interviewing them, attending their next talk on the topic, watching their previous recorded talks on YouTube or other platforms, and if needed, hiring them to provide specific analysis for your organization.

Synthesize internal knowledge about each driver

To understand how each driver may affect the organization, the team needs a detailed collective understanding of the organization and its operations to determine its exposure. If your organization has previously conducted assessments, given briefings, done risk analysis, business continuity analysis, or strategic planning analysis relating to a driver, collect and use it to understand the past, present, and potential future of it relative to the organization.

Also consider interviewing or re-interviewing any key people within the organization that may have knowledge of or experiences with a specific driver or drivers. In its *Explorer's Guide to Scenario Planning*, Shell noted that its leaders "consulted regularly with the senior stakeholders in Shell throughout the [scenario] building process."[10] One way to do this is to have team members feed recent scenario planning developments back to their own group or department, and bring their responses back to the project team for consideration. The added value of doing this is that when you come to present the draft scenarios, some of the details will not be completely foreign to them, and you may already have some buy-in since they contributed to them.

Scan research and media

It probably goes without saying that you should search online for recent research about each driver. A few times a week I type "climate change" into a search engine to look for research and news, and from my LinkedIn or Twitter accounts I post about climate trends affecting or potentially affecting organizations. I also currently follow @CeresNews and other good sources on Twitter (and the #ClimateChange hashtag), Reddit (the r/climate and r/climatechange sub-reddits), and subscribe to the *New York Times* "Climate Fwd:" newsletter, and other sources to keep up to date with recent climate-related trends as they relate (or could relate) to business. Another good resource is www.scholar.google.com. Many universities and research institutes also now have their own YouTube channel, for instance the University of California has a YouTube channel called University of California Television, on which you can watch many free lectures by scientists reporting the results of (and taking questions on) their own recent research on climate change and many other topics. Whatever your choice of search terms and social media, you will be able to use it to discover the latest research about each driver.

Interview major customers and suppliers

Many organizations are at least to some degree dependent on major suppliers or customers. As research proceeds, have someone collect questions and information about how key suppliers or large customers may be exposed to identified climate drivers, and organize interviews with representatives of those organizations to ask them about their own experiences with and knowledge about their own exposure to specific drivers. This is also an opportunity to involve account managers for those customers or suppliers in the project, as they will likely be the contact point. In the Introduction, I quoted from research by the Center for Climate and Energy Solutions[11] about organizations only being as resilient as their weakest link. To understand your organization's exposure to climate change drivers, you need to understand how exposed your suppliers and key customers are to them as well.

Consider broader economic drivers

Companies are economic entities, so even though the state of the economy might not (or might) be considered to be something directly related to climate change, the state of the economy and the business cycle at your time horizon will likely affect the shape of the future. Once you get to later stages of the scenario planning process, the state of the economy may also affect possible responses to the scenarios. Decide whether you want to incorporate a broad "state of the economy" driver into your list of driving forces even though you may not consider it directly related to climate change, or whether it is more appropriate to keep it separate, but keep it in mind when you are developing strategies later in the process.

Conduct deeper research where necessary

Aside from other research on each driver, Ralston and Wilson[12] gave some great advice about what to do when the driver workshop identifies key knowledge gaps: Have specific team members be responsible for further research on key questions. In relation to climate change, for example, someone might investigate how a specific driver may be affecting a competitor, or supplier, or specific geographic area. Have them prepare a 2–3 page briefing for the team, or a short presentation, so everyone can feed the information into their own research.

Rate and rank the driving forces

Scenario planning complements qualitative and quantitative information. The scenarios themselves (especially for teams undertaking scenario planning for the first time)[1] will likely include more qualitative than quantitative details, because they rely on the team's collective research and analysis, from which reasoning and patterns can be intuited.[13] However, the role of each driving force within those scenarios will be determined by a systematic ranking process that is heuristic but quantified. The purpose of systematically ranking the driving forces is to manage your optimism bias. If you or I simply chose which forces to include, research by Sharot[14] and Schoemaker[3] suggests that we will by default choose those that are more positive for the organization and overlook the less comfortable forces. Systematically rating the forces facilitates the production of a solid ranking, from which you will use the top two to shape the basic parameters of four scenarios. Many of the other forces will also appear in the scenarios, and others will be discarded. The ranking spreadsheet you are completing will facilitate the ranking for you, and in this section I will continue with the LocalBank example.

There are three aspects to ranking the forces: 1) Rating the uncertainty of each force out of 10; 2) Rating the potential impact of each force out of 10; and 3)

Multiplying the uncertainty and impact ratings for each force, and ranking the forces according to the total. Each step is covered below, and they can all be covered in a single workshop. The research done up to this point, especially to understand and map the geographic locations the organization's assets and operations, to understand the same for key suppliers and customers, and to understand the potential states of each driver at the time horizon will pay dividends when it comes to rating the drivers.

To complete the ranking, bring the team together in a 1–2 day workshop so everyone's research can be reported, discussed, and perhaps debated, and you can start putting numbers into the spreadsheet for uncertainty and impact. Individuals or teams responsible for researching the drivers should bring draft ratings for uncertainty and impact, and their notes and research materials to justify them. See Box 3.2, and further details below. The role of the facilitator or project lead at this point is to ensure that people have good reasons, or evidence, for the number they advocate for as a rating, but to also remain open to others' views and ideas.

BOX 3.2 CLIMATE DRIVER RATING AND RANKING WORKSHOP

As a structure for the workshop, and in consultation with any facilitator, consider the following elements:

- **Opening:** Introduce the aim and agenda of the workshop: To rate each driving force in terms of uncertainty and potential impact, and then to rank the set of forces. If relevant, also report any changes to the driver list that occurred since the last workshop as a result of research and driver specification. If time permits, you may be able to achieve more by combining this workshop with the next one to start developing the scenarios (see Chapter 4 for details).
- **Rate each driver on the list for uncertainty and potential impact:** See detailed instructions in this chapter.
- **Rank the list of forces:** See detailed instructions in this chapter. Report the two top-ranking forces that will drive scenario development.
- **Conclusion:** To conclude the workshop, summarize what has been achieved – a ranked list of driving forces from which the scenarios will be developed, or as far as you got in the process, and details of the next workshop to develop the scenarios.

Some scenario planners have rated driving forces according to uncertainty and importance[8] rather than uncertainty and impact. Since scenario planning for climate change requires the need to think about potential physical impacts, rating impact is appropriate. Rating impact will also help to avoid unexpected drivers being "normalized out of existence," as Karl Weick might put it.[15] In my own study of organizational responses to climate change,[16] I identified this normalizing tendency among decision-makers, as the physical impacts of extreme weather were perceived to be part of an anomalous weather pattern they assumed would return to normal, until they experienced what I called "climatic surprise,"[17] where weather events affected operations close to home, were perceived as less predictable, and challenged this assumption. The goal is to avoid normalizing anomalous weather events that research has linked to climate change.

It is also worth noting here that although you are quantifying the forces to some degree by applying ratings out of 10, it is only for the purpose of ranking them. A rating of 3, 7, or 9 for uncertainty or impact for a given force need only be justified to the scenario planning team and its audience. The ratings are a heuristic quantification of the team's collective interpretation of all the research done on the driving force. Determining the uncertainty and impact for each force can take time, and it is often done iteratively with specifying them.

Rate uncertainty

As Peter Schwartz[8] wrote, "freedom is the ability to act both with confidence and a full knowledge of uncertainty." To get to a point of acting with confidence in full knowledge of uncertainties, you will need to gain an in-depth understanding of "critical uncertainties"[3, 10] surrounding each driving force. You should have a sense of critical uncertainties from your understanding of the current state, historical trend, future projections, and dynamics of each driver, as well as your knowledge of the organization, its operations, and locations. Following is a list of sample questions to help you rate the uncertainty of each driving force now that you've done the basic research:

- What do we know and not know about what determines the historical, current, and future states of the driving force?
- What do we know and not know about its internal workings? For instance, is it cyclical, or does its current trend represent ongoing permanent change, or some combination of the two?
- What do we know and not know about the outcomes of historical trends, key events, disruptions in trend, and extremes?
- What do we know and not know about its current state?
- What do we know and not know about its plausible states and outcomes (including key events, disruptions in trend, and extremes) at the chosen time horizon?
- Overall, what are the most "critical uncertainties" of the driving force at the time horizon that could be difficult for our organization?

To begin answering these questions, it is crucial that you understand the difference between uncertainty and probability. In this method, you will examine the *uncertainty* surrounding a given force, but many people have probability ingrained in their thinking and assume they are interchangeable. Uncertainty is not probability, but they are related.

It is worthwhile reinforcing here the difference between scenario planning and risk management. The focus on uncertainty rather than probability is a key differentiator between scenario planning and risk management. If you were doing a long-term risk management plan, you could use the same drivers you are identifying here, and you would estimate probability and impact, rather than uncertainty and impact. Using the same multiplication method set out here in a risk management setting, you would develop a ranked list of risks starting with those that are highly probable and highly impactful; however, the list would continue to reinforce traditional strategizing approaches, because the list would be of more or less probable and impactful risks to a pre-determined singular view of the future. The list would not answer the question of "What might surprise us?" Scenario planning aims to prepare your organization for what might surprise it as well as what is thought will plausibly happen.

Using a scale from one to ten, you will rate the degree of *uncertainty* surrounding each driving force in relation to your organization at your chosen time horizon. For example, if research indicates that sea level rise will almost certainly occur in Boston at the time horizon, it would be allocated a low number for uncertainty for LocalBank (since it is almost certain to happen, you are confident about its probability of occurring). If sea level rise were almost certainly not going to occur at the time horizon, it would also be allocated a low number on the scale (since it is almost certain not to happen, you are confident about its probability of not occurring). However, if research indicates nothing about whether sea level rise might or might not occur at the time horizon, then LocalBank would rate uncertainty much higher, up to 10, because it cannot establish probability with any degree of confidence. Figure 3.1 illustrates the difference, and also shows the relationship between uncertainty and impact ratings, in that uncertainty about the nature of impacts can affect the uncertainty rating.

The scale is out of 10 to provide teams with a high degree of granularity. In previous workshops I have tested scales of 5 and 7, and people have sometimes found them to be too blunt for their purposes. Further, the scale begins at 1 and not zero, because you will be multiplying the ratings for uncertainty and impact, and any zero will unfairly negate the other number in the equation. Finally, I chose an even numbered scale to minimize people opting for a middle number as a compromise, but if it becomes necessary (if discussion and debate between a rating

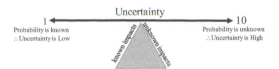

FIGURE 3.1 Uncertainty vs. probability

of 5 and 6 becomes intractable and this cannot be resolved by voting), then adding a decimal place is possible so you could opt for 5.5 out of 10.

As you rate the uncertainty of each driver out of 10, do your best given available information and research. For the purpose of this scenario planning method, you won't be using sophisticated software for Monte Carlo or stochastic modeling techniques. If, for example, you can only find 100-year IPCC projections for a given physical driver, or a 10-year projection for a particular technology driver, interpolate or extrapolate from that projection to a figure that is useful for your time horizon. Your aim is to get to a point where your team can understand the numbers assigned and justify them to your audience.

When you are ready to rate the level of uncertainty for a driver, put a number into the uncertainty column of the spreadsheet, and be prepared to justify it to the rest of the scenario planning team. After you have rated the uncertainty you are ready to rate the impact. You may iterate between rating uncertainty and impact as you investigate the impacts more deeply and realize there is less or more uncertainty surrounding impacts than first thought.

Rate potential impact

Rating the potential impact of a driver means assuming it will affect your organization at the chosen time horizon. As was the case when rating the uncertainty, team members will make good use of their research in this step. The rating system is the same for impact as it was for uncertainty, and the objective is to apply an impact rating out of 10.

As you assess impacts, consider both plausible quantitative and qualitative aspects of material impacts. For instance, you would consider how it might impact "Input costs, Operating costs, Revenues, Supply chain, Business interruption, Timing," as suggested by the TCFD.[1] Qualitative aspects of impacts include answering questions like exactly how could it affect the organization (i.e. by what process)?, or how might a driver affect relationships with stakeholders (e.g. how might it affect how your organization relates to the community in which it operates?), the culture of your organization, branding, leadership, and communication styles, etc.?

It is also important to return to your list of key stakeholders and assess how material the driver might be for them (especially key suppliers, customers, and infrastructure providers). You may also see the need to iterate back to refine your list of key stakeholders if you identify other stakeholders through your impact analysis. It is also not unusual to revisit how you have specified the force, and to refine how the impacts of a force are written into the spreadsheet.

I noted earlier that you may notice some interaction between uncertainty and impact. Specifically, if after you have done your impact analysis there is uncertainty about a driver's impacts on your organization, it may cause you to raise the uncertainty rating for that driver. For example, if sea level change is certain for LocalBank, but the exact amount of sea level change is uncertain, it may increase the uncertainty rating for sea level change to account for the remaining uncertainty of impact. This is shown in Figure 3.1 using the "known impacts" and "unknown impacts" on either side of the triangle base.

It is also important to distinguish the potential impacts of a force on your organization from how your organization might respond. In this step you should only identify how a force might impact your organization for the purpose of rating impacts out of 10. It is common for people to start thinking about what the organization might be forced to do, or what it could do in advance of the time horizon to mitigate the issue. To rate impact efficiently, assume that your organization would continue along its current strategic trajectory without taking onboard the driving force (unless that driving force is already accounted for in its strategic plan or other disclosures). For example, if LocalBank had already identified that sea level rise could have material impacts for properties used as collateral in its loan portfolio, it would consider any strategies already in place, but leave further potential responses out of scope until Step 4 of the method when strategies are developed. This is another point at which people can slip into strategizing mode, so as noted earlier, avoid developing strategies at this point that would be focused on a single driver, but take a note of your ideas so you can flesh them out later when you have the bigger picture of the scenarios.

When you are ready to rate the level of impact for a driver, put a number into the impact column of the spreadsheet, and be prepared to justify it to the scenario planning team.

By the time you have finished rating the uncertainty and impact of each driving force, the output will look something like that illustrated in Table 3.5, which shows the uncertainty and impact ratings for each of LocalBank's driving forces (note that the uncertainty and impact ratings are completely arbitrary in this example and you should not rely on them for your own analysis). The descriptions of each force are also more detailed. Resist calculating the total until you have all your ratings done to ensure you are letting the numbers speak for themselves, and you are not pressuring any driver to rise to the top of the ranking.

Complete the ranking

Ranking the forces places all the driving forces on an even playing field for the important step of determining which drivers will become the parameters of your scenarios, which drivers should appear in all scenarios because they almost certainly will happen and are of some consequence, and which can be disregarded because they almost certainly will not happen or after examination have been found to have little impact.

After you have rated uncertainty and impact, completing the ranking is a straightforward process of multiplying uncertainty and impact to arrive at the total for each driving force, and then sorting the list of the drivers from highest to lowest according to their total score. In our running LocalBank example, this would result in the order depicted in Table 3.6.

While ranking is a simple mathematical process, it is usually a step that challenges people's assumptions, and therefore should be done in a group setting. Challenges

TABLE 3.5 Rated list of climate change drivers for LocalBank

Ranking the driving forces

Driving force	A. Uncertainty rating*	B. Impact rating**	Total (A×B)
Extreme weather events: By [year of 25-year time horizon], extreme weather (thunderstorms, hurricanes, nor'easters) will increase in intensity and incidence, significantly affecting operations, and causing collateral property damage, coastal erosion, and cause people to move away every 3–4 years.	5.0	5.0	
Sea level change: By [year of 25-year time horizon], sea levels will rise by 12″ in Boston, causing regular flooding at high tide, and exacerbating storm surge damage and property damage, causing people to move away. (relates to extreme weather)	3.0	7.0	
Infrastructure adaptation: By [year of 25-year time horizon], there will be significant progress by City and State to adapt infrastructure and landscape to rising sea levels and extreme weather that will reduce property damage and human migration. (relates to sea level rise, extreme weather)	5.0	6.0	
Carbon emissions policies: By [year of 25-year time horizon], national policies to curb carbon emissions will be in place, and State policies will be more stringent.	7.0	2.0	
Precipitation: By [year of 25-year time horizon], more precipitation will fall as rain (and heavy rain) and less as snow, leading to less snow cover and more flooding. (relates to temperature rise)	5.0	8.0	
Ambient temperature over land: By [year of 25-year time horizon], temperature will rise by 1.5°F and Boston will experience more heatwaves, affecting customer health, and working conditions on construction sites of property tied to real estate and construction loans.	3.0	8.0	
Ocean temperature: By [year of 25-year time horizon], ocean temperature will rise by 2°F, keeping Atlantic hurricanes alive as they progress up the coast to Massachusetts. (relates to extreme weather)	3.0	6.0	

*A. Uncertainty about whether it will happen out of 10: 1 – it will certainly happen or certainly not happen → 10 – it is highly uncertain whether it will happen or not.
**B. Impact if it happens out of 10: 1 – no material impact to the organization → 10 – very significant material impact to the organization.

TABLE 3.6 Ranked list of climate change drivers for LocalBank

Ranking the driving forces

Driving force	A. Uncertainty rating*	B. Impact rating**	Total (A×B)
Precipitation: By [year of 25-year time horizon], more precipitation will fall as rain (and heavy rain) and less as snow, leading to less snow cover and more flooding. (relates to temperature rise)	5.0	8.0	40.00
Infrastructure adaptation: By [year of 25-year time horizon], there will be significant progress by City and State to adapt infrastructure and landscape to rising sea levels and extreme weather that will reduce property damage and human migration. (relates to sea level rise, extreme weather)	5.0	6.0	30.00
Extreme weather events: By [year of 25-year time horizon], extreme weather (thunderstorms, hurricanes, nor'easters) will increase in intensity and incidence, significantly affecting operations, and causing collateral property damage, coastal erosion, and cause people to move away every 3–4 years.	5.0	5.0	25.00
Ambient temperature over land: By [year of 25-year time horizon], temperature will rise by 1.5°F and Boston will experience more heatwaves, affecting customer health, and working conditions on construction sites of property tied to real estate and construction loans.	3.0	8.0	24.00
Sea level change: By [year of 25-year time horizon], sea levels will rise by 12″ in Boston, causing regular flooding at high tide, and exacerbating storm surge damage and property damage, causing people to move away. (relates to extreme weather)	3.0	7.0	21.00
Ocean temperature: By [year of 25-year time horizon], ocean temperature will rise by 2°F, keeping Atlantic hurricanes alive as they progress up the coast to Massachusetts. (relates to extreme weather)	3.0	6.0	18.00
Carbon emissions policies: By [year of 25-year time horizon], national policies to curb carbon emissions will be in place, and State policies will be more stringent.	7.0	2.0	14.00

*A. Uncertainty about whether it will happen out of 10: 1 – it will certainly happen or certainly not happen → 10 – it is highly uncertain whether it will happen or not.

**B. Impact if it happens out of 10: 1 – no material impact to the organization → 10 – very significant material impact to the organization.

may arise as certain drivers that were expected to rise to the top of the ranking did not, while the method suggests that other drivers, which didn't seem intuitively important, are now determining the shape of the rest of the project. It is important at this point to let the numbers speak for themselves, since a great deal of research has been done to generate them, and by many people. If, after multiplying uncertainty and impact, a force rises to the top of the ranking that you weren't expecting, or would have preferred not be there, let it stay there. Biases can come into play at this juncture, as team members want go back and re-produce research to alter the ranking to something that caters to their optimism bias, or otherwise concurs with their expectations. If your analysis has been rigorous and discussed with the whole team, there is no need to question or redo it simply because the results are surprising. The ranking can surprise people and challenge their assumptions about what forces they believed would rank highly, and this is the very point of scenario planning. Have faith in your research and take the ranking as it is.

Other drivers in your ranking will also be needed for the scenarios, so being a lower-ranking driver does not necessarily mean it will be taken out of scope. For instance, those forces that were deemed highly certain will appear lower on the ranking and will become attributes of every scenario. These forces are similar to what Wack,[18] Schwartz,[8] and Shell[10] scenario planners called "predetermined elements" – aspects of the future that are certain, or perhaps the impacts are not rated highly, but still need to be accounted for.

To conclude this step, you should update any project documentation you have with your ranked list of drivers. You now have the foundations of the scenarios you will develop in Step 3: A ranked list of drivers, first- and second-ranking drivers that will shape the scenarios, and lower-ranking drivers that will flesh out the details of each scenario. These are based on rich research completed for each driver that will add nuance to the scenarios, and bring them to life.

References

1 TCFD. 2016. *The Use of Scenario Analysis in Disclosure of Climate-Related Risks and Opportunities.* Financial Stability Board Task Force on Climate-Related Financial Disclosures. https://www.fsb-tcfd.org/publications/technical-supplement/#, accessed 20 Feb 2017.

2 Wilkinson, A. and R. Kupers. 2013. Living in the futures, *Harvard Business Review*, 91/5: 118–127.

3 Schoemaker, P.J.H. 1995. Scenario planning: A tool for strategic thinking, *Sloan Management Review*, 36/2: 25–40.

4 *MBA Boost.* 2018. STEEP analysis tool. https://www.mbaboost.com/steep-analysis-tool/, accessed 16 July 2018.

5 IPCC. 2014. *Climate Change 2014: Synthesis Report. Contribution of Working Groups I, II and III to the Fifth Assessment Report of the Intergovernmental Panel on Climate Change,* ed. R.K. Pachauri and L.A. Meyer. Geneva: IPCC.

6 IPCC. 2014. *Climate Change 2014: Impacts, Adaptation, and Vulnerability. Part A: Global and Sectoral Aspects. Contribution of Working Group II to the Fifth Assessment Report of the Intergovernmental Panel on Climate Change.* Cambridge & New York: Cambridge University Press.

7 IPCC. 2014. *Climate Change 2014: Impacts, Adaptation, and Vulnerability. Part B: Regional Aspects. Contribution of Working Group II to the Fifth Assessment Report of the Intergovernmental Panel on Climate Change*, ed. V.R. Barros, et al. Cambridge & New York: Cambridge University Press.

8 Schwartz, P. 1996. *The Art of the Long View: Planning for the Future in an Uncertain World*. New York: Doubleday.

9 Shugar, D.H., J.J. Clague, J.L. Best, C. Schoof, M.J. Willis, L. Copland and G.H. Roe. 2017. River piracy and drainage basin reorganization led by climate-driven glacier retreat. *Nature Geoscience*, 10, 370–375. http://dx.doi.org/10.1038/ngeo2932, accessed 28 April 2017.

10 Shell. 2008. *Scenarios: An Explorer's Guide. Exploring the Future*. The Hague: Shell International BV.

11 C2ES. 2015. *Weathering the Next Storm: A Closer Look at Business Resilience*. Center for Climate and Energy Solutions.

12 Ralston, B. and I. Wilson. 2006. *The Scenario-Planning Handbook: A Practitioner's Guide to Developing and Using Scenarios to Direct Strategy in Today's Uncertain Times*. Mason, OH: Thomson/South-Western.

13 Lindgren, M. and H. Bandhold. 2009. *Scenario Planning: The Link Between Future and Strategy*. 2nd edn. Houndmills, UK: Palgrave Macmillan.

14 Sharot, T. 2012. Tali Sharot: The optimism bias. *TED*. http://www.ted.com/talks/tali_sharot_the_optimism_bias#t-1008491, accessed 2 February 2017.

15 Weick, K.E. 2005. Managing the unexpected: Complexity as distributed sensemaking, in *Uncertainty and Surprise in Complex Systems: Questions on Working with the Unexpected*, ed. R.R. McDaniel and D.J. Driebe. Berlin: Springer. pp. 51–66.

16 Haigh, N.L. 2008. *A Study of Organisational Strategy in Response to Climate Change Issues*. Brisbane: The University of Queensland.

17 Haigh, N.L. and A. Griffiths. 2012. Surprise as a catalyst for including climatic change in the strategic environment, *Business & Society*, 51/1: 89–120.

18 Wack, P. 1985. Scenarios: Uncharted waters ahead, *Harvard Business Review*, 63/5: 73–89.

4

STEP 3: DEVELOP THE SCENARIOS

Peter Schwartz[1] described scenarios as stories that are

> ... carefully researched, full of relevant detail, oriented toward real-life decisions, and designed (one hopes) to bring forward surprises and unexpected leaps of understanding.

Each scenario will become a compelling and vivid "what if" story[2, 3] with "a start, middle, and end of what happened and how,"[4] to build a set of relevant, plausible futures that are easily communicated.[3, 5]

Many scenario planners, including myself, recommend developing the scenarios in two stages. In the first stage, you will develop initial draft scenarios; what others have called "first-generation,"[6] "simple," or "learning"[7] scenarios. In the second stage, you will develop a final set of detailed scenarios. Step 3 concludes once the final four scenarios are developed, and this will set you up for strategizing in Step 4.

Now that you have a ranked list of forces, in this step you will use the common scenario planning technique of developing four scenarios using the two highest ranking forces as axes; creating a scenario matrix.[1, 8, 9] After studying the forces individually up to this point, you will now examine how various combinations of the forces could interact in the four alternate scenarios.

Many scenario planners, including myself, also advise keeping the maximum number of scenarios at four so you and your audience can digest them:[1, 6, 10, 11] "While there is an almost infinite number of possible scenarios, organizations can use a limited number of scenarios to provide the desired variety."[10] Your scenarios need to draw your audience in, so it's important that they be digestible, as well as engaging the priorities and assumptions of your audience, even if they will challenge those assumptions.

You also do not want to develop fewer than four scenarios. Four is a good number, because it presents decision-makers with a variety of plausible futures, and prevents them from trying to find a middle ground if given three plausible scenarios, or the positive scenario if only two were presented.[1, 12] Four scenarios will help your audience get to a point of not being invested in any one future, so they can prepare for them all.

Creating the scenarios is not a trivial job. To develop engaging, surprising, challenging scenarios, they need to have a few key attributes, which the TCFD[10] articulates exceptionally well in relation to climate change. Keep these in mind as you develop your scenarios:

1. *Plausible. The events in the scenario should be possible and the narrative credible (i.e., the descriptions of what happened, and why and how it happened, should be believable).*
2. *Distinctive. Each scenario should focus on a different combination of the key factors. Scenarios should be clearly differentiated from each other in structure and in message, not variations on a single theme. Multiple scenarios should be used to explore how different permutations and/or temporal developments of the same key factors can yield very different outcomes.*
3. *Consistent. Each scenario should have strong internal logic. The goal of scenario analysis is to explore the way that factors interact, and each action should have a reaction. Neither actors nor external factors should completely overturn the evidence of current trends and positions unless logical explanations for those changes are a central part of the scenario.*
4. *Relevant. Each scenario, and the set of scenarios taken as a whole, should contribute specific insights into the future that relate to strategic and/or financial implications of climate-related risks and opportunities.*
5. *Challenging. Scenarios should challenge conventional wisdom and simplistic assumptions about the future. When thinking about the major sources of uncertainty, scenarios should try to explore alternatives that will significantly alter the basis for business-as-usual assumptions.*

Draft initial scenarios

Developing the set of draft scenarios provides the first opportunity to consider how various forces might interact, how your organization and its stakeholders may be affected, and how stakeholders may respond. Your draft scenarios will be presented to a broader audience for feedback.

Developing draft scenarios can be done using a mix of individual and group work. Hold a scenario development workshop to communicate the scenario parameters, decide or communicate who will lead the development of each scenario, and begin developing the scenarios. Box 4.1 outlines a potential workshop agenda.

BOX 4.1 DRAFT SCENARIO DEVELOPMENT WORKSHOP

As a structure for the workshop, and in consultation with any facilitator, consider covering the following elements over 1–2 days:

- **Opening:** Introduce the aim and agenda of the workshop: To start developing draft scenarios based on the ranked list of forces.
- **Review the scenario baseline formed by mid- and low-ranking drivers.** See details in this chapter.
- **Review the scenario framework formed by the two top-ranking drivers.** See details in this chapter.
- **Start developing draft scenarios:** In break-out groups or predefined teams for each scenario, spend a morning or afternoon session drafting the details of each scenario. Further details about this are included in this chapter. Have each break-out present their working notes or draft of their scenario to the team and get initial feedback.
- **Conclusion:** To conclude the workshop, summarize what has been achieved – establishment of scenario teams, if needed, and starting drafts of scenarios, or as far as you got in the process. Provide details of the next workshop.

One of the main strengths of scenario planning – lack of need for consensus – is important in this step, since the scenarios will likely present what may be seen as improbable sequences of events, and may highlight issues that are sources of debate. An external facilitator can be useful here to ensure discussion is not dominated by the more powerful, more opinionated or vocal actors in the room, or as Shell noted, "those who have a natural desire to come up with answers quickly."[3] Facilitating inclusive discussion will build rigor into the process if everyone has a voice to generate ideas, question their own and others' ideas, and build on the knowledge being generated. As Schoemaker[7] said, "[t]he overall purpose is to build a shared framework for strategic thinking that encourages diversity and sharper perceptions about external changes and opportunities."

The next steps will help you create the basic framework of your scenarios using the two highest-ranking drivers, and determine which of your other lower-ranking drivers will be included in the scenarios.

Create a scenario framework using the two highest-ranking drivers

First, develop the scenario frameworks based on the two highest-ranking forces. It's at this point where the method imposes probability on the two highest ranking forces to provide the scaffolding of four plausible futures. As Figure 4.1 illustrates, these scenarios are clearly differentiated.

For LocalBank, the scenario framework would look like that depicted in Figure 4.2.

The axes in Figure 4.1 are binary, in that a given force is deemed to either occur and have material impacts for the organization, or not, and this makes the scenarios deliberately incompatible. If the team decides that the driving forces for your organization should be considered on a scale from less to more impactful, rather from a binary standpoint, another way to approach Figure 4.1 is to develop scenarios that sit

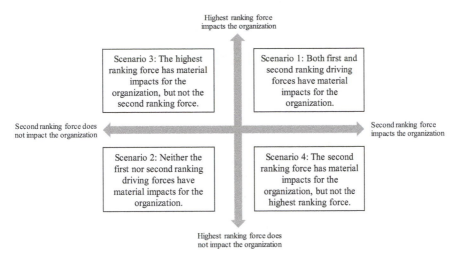

FIGURE 4.1 Scenario framework

across several quadrants. If you take this approach, ensure you are preserving the distinctiveness of each scenario by not letting them overlap on the framework.

Each scenario is driven by a different combination of the two top-ranking driving forces, so while there may be similar reasons a certain force did or did not affect the organization from one scenario to the next, the combination of forces is different from one scenario to the next. These differences may yield different potential impacts, different stakeholder responses, etc.

Below is a basic description of each scenario. You can start writing the rough story of each scenario as you go by starting with a statement as simple as "In [time horizon year], [organization] is experiencing the effects of ...." It does not need to be perfect. You will improve the wording later as you edit. An excellent technique

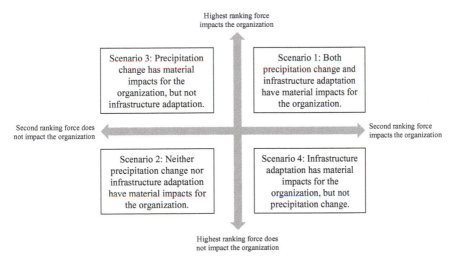

FIGURE 4.2 Scenario framework for LocalBank

offered by Woody Wade is to include a plausible but "fictional chronology of events"[9] from present day to the time horizon. Another idea, from Paul Schoemaker, is to write "imaginary newspaper headlines to characterize the events and driving forces of each scenario."[13]

Scenario 1

Scenario 1 assumes that both the first and second ranking driving forces occur and have material impacts for the organization. I mentioned in the previous chapter that climate change drivers often seem to bring more potential threats than opportunities for most organizations. If your organization's highest ranking drivers are predominantly negative, especially if the forces interact and exacerbate each other's impacts, this scenario will likely be the worst case scenario.

Scenario 2

Scenario 2 assumes that neither the first nor second-ranking forces occur or have material impacts for the organization. Many people incorrectly assume that Scenario 2 is the easier to prepare, because it looks like business-as-usual. In reality, as much research is needed to make this scenario plausible as any other.

Further, Scenario 2 may not be the most surprising scenario, but there are two important reasons for keeping it. First, Pierre Wack[6] and Peter Schwartz[1] argue, and I agree, that it potentially represents the "official future" currently assumed in strategic plans, and therefore is less threatening to anyone who is uncomfortable with the scenario planning process. As Ged Davis, previous head of Shell Scenario Planning, was quoted as saying: "All successful scenarios are focused in the sense that they are derived from a fundamental consideration of their client's dilemmas and needs."[5] Comfort with the process may be a need of your audience, and this scenario could provide it.

Another reason Scenario 2 is important is that it can help demonstrate the limitations of rational single-future strategizing. Presenting this scenario within the set of four scenarios highlights that the organization faces multiple plausible futures, not just one, and while the current vision and strategic plan may have a place in those futures, it also may not.

In relation to climate change, Scenario 2 often appears to portray a stable and unsurprising future; however, explaining why physical climate change forces do not occur or do not impact the organization can be challenging. You can examine technology forecasts and even dabble in science fiction to explore potential technological developments by the horizon date, as well as climate skeptic arguments that are grounded in climate science, as long as each scenario remains plausible.

Scenario 3

Scenario 3 assumes the highest ranking force occurs and has material impacts for the organization, but not the second ranking force. The starting story you draft explaining the impact of the highest ranking force may be similar to that you identified in Scenario 1. Similarly, the starting explanation of why the second-ranking force does not impact the organization may be similar to that you identified in Scenario 2. However, when taken together, an entirely different explanation may be required to explain this combination of forces, particularly if they interact. I only mention borrowing explanations about individual drivers from other scenarios to help you start writing and thinking about this scenario. This new combination of forces will also impact the organization in different ways than the previous two scenarios.

Scenario 4

Finally, Scenario 4 assumes that the highest ranking force does not occur or have material impacts for the organization. The second-ranking force, however, does. Similar to Scenario 3, your starting explanation of why the second ranking force has impact may be similar to that in Scenario 1, while your starting explanation of why the first-ranking force has no impact could be borrowed from Scenario 2, but together, this new combination of forces is qualitatively different and requires a new story.

Next, before you start developing the detailed narrative for each scenario, identify which of your lower-ranked forces will plausibly affect the organization at the time horizon.

Identify certainties to create a scenario baseline

The low-ranking drivers that were rated higher on impact but low on uncertainty because they will almost certainly occur should become a baseline for all four of your draft scenarios. These forces appeared lower in the ranking because they were deemed certain to have some kind of direct or indirect impact on the organization at the time horizon. For LocalBank, Table 4.1 shows that these drivers are potentially: Extreme weather, land temperature, sea level change, and ocean temperature. Carbon emissions policies are not included, because the impact rating was low.

Move on to your mid-ranking forces. Although mid-ranking forces do not rank highly enough to define your scenarios, they are uncertain and impactful enough to be relevant to your scenario planning project. Work through the list of mid-ranking forces, and decide whether to assume each mid-ranking force should be included in the baseline, or whether it is more useful to consider it within only some scenarios. If any mid-ranking force could have significant material implications for the organization, especially if it interacts with other drivers (more on interaction below), include it in the baseline. At this stage including it is a no-regrets decision, because you aren't making decisions right now about what to do, you are only in the starting stages of drafting initial scenarios that will be further crafted as the method proceeds. For example, Table 4.1 indicates that extreme weather is a mid-ranking force rated five for both uncertainty and impact.

TABLE 4.1 Ranked list of climate change drivers for LocalBank

Ranking the driving forces

Driving force	A. Uncertainty rating*	B. Impact rating**	Total (A×B)
Precipitation: By [year of 25-year time horizon], more precipitation will fall as rain (and heavy rain) and less as snow, leading to less snow cover and more flooding. (relates to temperature rise)	5.0	8.0	40.00
Infrastructure adaptation: By [year of 25-year time horizon], there will be significant progress by City and State to adapt infrastructure and landscape to rising sea levels and extreme weather that will reduce property damage and human migration. (relates to sea level rise, extreme weather)	5.0	6.0	30.00
Extreme weather events: By [year of 25-year time horizon], extreme weather (thunderstorms, hurricanes, nor'easters) will increase in intensity and incidence, significantly affecting operations, and causing collateral property damage, coastal erosion, and cause people to move away every 3–4 years.	5.0	5.0	25.00
Ambient temperature over land: By [year of 25-year time horizon], temperature will rise by 1.5°F and Boston will experience more heatwaves, affecting customer health, and working conditions on construction sites of property tied to real estate and construction loans.	3.0	8.0	24.00
Sea level change: By [year of 25-year time horizon], sea levels will rise by 12″ in Boston, causing regular flooding at high tide, and exacerbating storm surge damage and property damage, causing people to move away. (relates to extreme weather)	3.0	7.0	21.00
Ocean temperature: By [year of 25-year time horizon], ocean temperature will rise by 2°F, keeping Atlantic hurricanes alive as they progress up the coast to Massachusetts. (relates to extreme weather)	3.0	6.0	18.00
Carbon emissions policies: By [year of 25-year time horizon], national policies to curb carbon emissions will be in place, and State policies will be more stringent.	7.0	2.0	14.00

*A. Uncertainty about whether it will happen out of 10: 1 – it will certainly happen or certainly not happen → 10 – it is highly uncertain whether it will happen or not.
**B. Impact if it happens out of 10: 1 – no material impact to the organization → 10 – very significant material impact to the organization.

Including extreme weather in the scenario baseline is a no-regrets decision, since it is only helping LocalBank consider the impacts of extreme weather at this point, and is not dictating any particular response.

The scenario baseline of certain (and some slightly less certain) forces and impacts recognizes, as Schoemaker[7] put it "that our world possesses considerable momentum and continuity." Identifying certainties as a baseline for all scenarios may also be important for people who are uncomfortable with the scenario planning process, since these drivers are more likely to include known issues.

Write a scenario baseline narrative, or story, and add that baseline to each scenario. Begin to write a story about the path of each driving force from present day to the scenario time horizon. The research you conducted for these drivers will indicate the plausible state of each at the time horizon. In your baseline, include details of how it differs from the present day, the point at which it began to diverge from present day, and why it diverged. You can start with the same simple phrase mentioned above, and improve your wording later: "In [time horizon year], [organization] is experiencing the effects of ...."

Develop a draft narrative for each scenario

Scenario planning now becomes a thought project 25 years into the future, or however many years your time horizon dictates. You will envision how a particular scenario might unfold, how it might impact the organization and key stakeholders, and how stakeholders might respond. Good scenarios challenge managerial and organizational assumptions by requiring explanations to situations that may seem improbable or counter-intuitive.

Every detail of each scenario requires careful construction, but the introduction needs special care, because you are asking audience members – directors, board members, employees, investors, etc. – to suspend their biases, assumptions, and any disbelief, so they can engage with you in this thought project. The best scenarios are "both plausible and surprising,"[1] and the surprises need to be introduced with convincing plausibility.

By adding your starting baseline story to the scenarios you started about the top-ranking forces in each scenario, you will now begin to craft a story for each scenario that will bring to life all the images, facts, figures, insights, and results of your research. Developing the narrative of each scenario helps you to engage decision-makers by capturing their imagination, and helps communicate the scenarios to your stakeholders. As you do this, ensure you address the attributes in the TCFD's[10] scenario attribute list at the beginning of the chapter. In particular, address the "relevant" attribute, because it will help you develop scenarios that are plausible, focused on the organization and industry in which it operates, and make the strategic implications evident. This will facilitate better feedback, and in Step 4 better strategies.[3]

Once you draft each scenario, leave it for a day or two, or longer, and come back to it with fresh eyes, so your sub-conscious has time to work in the background on plausible explanations. Below are a few tips as you begin to draft the story of each scenario.

Describe how each force happened, or not, and its impacts, at the time horizon

Each scenario must "grow logically (in a cause/effect way) from the past and the present and reflect current knowledge."[8] The story of each scenario should answer questions, like "How would the world get from here to there?" and "What events might be necessary to make the end point of the scenario plausible?"[1] You've just analyzed each force and considered how and why each force may or may not happen, and how it might or might not affect the organization, because you assigned specific ratings to rank it. Use this analysis in combination with your imagination to explain why it happened or did not happen at the time horizon, and what impacts it brought.

As Paul Hawken, James Ogilvy, and Peter Schwartz mentioned in their book, *Seven Tomorrows: Toward a Voluntary History*, each scenario is "a work of imagination with some novelistic touches added to color what might otherwise be drab trend projections."[14] Use the same techniques you used when writing the scenario baseline to begin writing your scenarios.

Consider what the plot of each scenario might be. In *The Art of the Long View*,[1] Schwartz identifies several potential plots, including a zero sum plot called Winners and Losers, another called Challenge and Response, where challenges are learning opportunities, and a slow but steady plot called Evolution. Or, maybe a combination of these or other plots might be in play. Use your imagination.

Describe how the forces could interact

Up to this point, the focus has been predominantly on analyzing single driving forces; however, interactions between driving forces may create important "joint impacts" that become crucial, and even "give rise to a scenario."[7] Examine whether, and if so how, the top-ranking and baseline forces could interact, and how any interactions could mitigate or exacerbate direct or indirect impacts. As Shell[3] advised in its scenario guide, ensure you address those dynamics and impacts that your key audience members see as most salient, even if it is to challenge their assumptions.

For LocalBank, the scenario baseline includes extreme weather, increasing land temperature, sea level change, and rising ocean temperature, while top-ranking drivers are precipitation change and infrastructure adaptation. The ability of the City and State to adapt local energy, water, coastal, and emergency infrastructure, as well as the landscape, could interact with many of these forces. For instance, if more precipitation will fall as rain instead of snow, and more rain could fall generally, then the need for snow plowing could drop, while inland flooding, riverbank erosion, and damage to properties, energy infrastructure, and emergency service infrastructure could increase if water drainage is not adapted. These impacts could devalue properties that LocalBank holds as collateral. Other inter-actions surround extreme weather, which relates to ocean temperature (since hurricanes are fed by warm water), sea level change (together they produce higher storm surge), precipitation (which accompanies extreme weather), and infrastructure adaptation (which could mitigate storm surge and property damage). Impacts from these dynamics could seriously affect property value, and put construction and property development, thus property development loans, at risk. While I haven't considered all the interactions between LocalBank's forces, these examples underscore the importance of considering plausible interactions between the driving forces.

A final note on interactions: If interacting forces present significant new uncer-tainties, the uncertainty rating of those driving forces may need to be revised, causing some iteration back to step two for those forces – this is depicted in the Introduction Figure 0.1 with the arrow from Step 3 back to Step 2. If this occurs, consult with the project team about whether the project needs to iterate back through the ranking process to confirm or alter the two highest ranking forces, and work back through the method to return to this point.

Discard remaining forces

Wack[12] noted that decision-makers often ask about what to leave out, because they want to ensure that in years to come, people will look back and feel the scenarios prepared them and did not miss anything important. Discuss any remaining driving forces that have not yet been incorporated, with a view to set-ting them aside, at least for the time being. Since these forces have low combined uncertainty and impact, their use for the scenario planning project is questionable. If the team struggles to set some drivers aside, know that they can always be brought back in at a later stage, and that the issue of overlooking drivers can be addressed by repeating the scenario planning project at regular intervals, which is discussed in the Step 4 of the method.

Consider the nature of the industry and competitor environments under each scenario

If you have followed the process up to this point, you have the basis of four sce-nario narratives. The next topic to consider is how your industry and competitor environments would look under each scenario. What impacts would the scenario have on them? You may have already answered parts of these questions as you completed previous research on the drivers and scenarios, depending on your focal question, especially if your drivers originate in the industry or competitor envir-onments. If your scenarios mainly contain forces that relate to the general envir-onment – STEEP categories discussed in previous chapters – now is the time to consider how each scenario could affect the industry environment.

If you have studied business before, you'll probably be quite familiar with Porter's five forces framework[15] to analyze the industry environment. First published in the *Harvard Business Review* in 1979, Porter's five forces framework continues to be a useful framework to answer questions about the nature of an industry. For those of you who need more background, Harvard Business School Professor Michael Porter argued that the state and nature of competition in any industry relies on five "contending forces" spread among industry actors. These forces are listed and defined below in Porter's words, along with some questions for you to consider as you write more about the industry environment into your scenarios:

1 Threat of new entrants

The seriousness of the threat of entry depends on the barriers present and on the reaction from existing competitors that the entrant can expect. If barriers to entry are high and a newcomer can expect sharp retaliation from the entrenched competitors, obviously he will not pose a serious threat of entering.[15]

Would your climate change scenarios raise entry barriers to your industry and deter new competitors, or lower barriers and attract new competitors?

2 Bargaining power of suppliers

Suppliers can exert bargaining power on participants in an industry by raising prices or reducing the quality of purchased goods and services. Powerful suppliers can thereby squeeze profitability out of an industry unable to recover cost increases in its own prices.[15]

Would your climate change scenarios increase or decrease the bargaining power of your suppliers?

3 Bargaining power of customers

Customers likewise can force down prices, demand higher quality or more service, and play competitors off against each other—all at the expense of industry profits.[15]

Would your climate change scenarios increase or decrease the bargaining power of your customers?

4 Threat of substitute products

By placing a ceiling on prices it can charge, substitute products or services limit the potential of an industry.[15]

Would your climate change scenarios increase or decrease the number of substitute products available or the prices they command?

5 Rivalry among current competitors

> *Rivalry among existing competitors takes the familiar form of jockeying for position—using tactics like price competition, product introduction, and advertising slugfests.*[15]

Would your climate change scenarios increase or decrease the amount of rivalry in your industry? How would each scenario affect your competitors, suppliers and customers, or other key industry stakeholders, and how might they respond? In his description of Shell's scenario planning, Pierre Wack[6] reported that the scenario team reflected on how each oil-producing and oil-consuming country would likely respond to each scenario, and this built an understanding of each country's resources and capabilities. This requires a detailed understanding of each key stakeholder's strategies, resources and capabilities, and any response to similar previous issues. This also requires empathy for these stakeholders, to understand their world view and what logic might drive their potential responses.

Overall, ask yourself whether each scenario would make your industry a more attractive or less attractive one in which to compete.

Determine the impact of scenarios on core capabilities

In his paper published in *International Studies of Management & Organization*,[16] University of Pennsylvania Professor Paul Schoemaker suggests looking inside the organization to identify its core capabilities to identify how your scenarios may affect them.

Core capabilities are those capabilities that distinguish organizations from their competitors, and are the foundation of their competitive advantage.[17] Core capabilities emerge over time as an organization learns what works best for it and its markets,[17] and core capabilities will ideally have some synergy within the organization by serving multiple markets, products, or business units.[16] One might, for example, argue that Shell has a core capability in scenario planning. Many other organizations and consulting firms have now developed scenario planning capabilities; though it is still built into Shell's organizational brand, because the capability has built up over decades.

To identify core capabilities, identify things the organization does well, that are, as Schoemaker[16] mentions, unique, important, under the organization's control, durable, and have the ability to help the organization generate profit. As you look for core capabilities, you might also consider what Professor Dorothy Leonard of Harvard Business School calls "core rigidities."[18] Core rigidities are the negative flipside of core capabilities, in that the focus and energy directed towards them can impede an organization's ability to innovate, because they can create inertia. The underlying task here is to identify the core capabilities (or rigidities) of your organization, and as Schoemaker suggests, map whether each scenario will have positive, negative, or neutral impacts on them.[16]

Focusing on the team's collective insights[3] about how each scenario could affect your core capabilities, and the broader organization, will also help you consider how each scenario might affect key performance metrics, assets, products, or markets. This will help you explain the scenarios using language that makes sense to decision-makers. Schoemaker's notion of "disciplined imagination"[16] becomes important as you write stories that depict how each scenario could unfold, what it could look like at the time horizon, and how it could affect your organization and its key stakeholders.

Look for potential opportunities as well as potential threats so you can flesh the scenarios out with rich details. If you feel it might be helpful, write the scenarios in the present tense, as if you had traveled through time to the time horizon and are reporting back to the present day. Strike a balance between expanding your thinking and "drifting into unbridled science fiction."[7] You can be encouraged by Peter Schwartz here, who mentioned that

> [a]nyone can create scenarios ... but it will be much easier if you are willing to encourage your own imagination, novelty, and even a sense of the absurd – as well as your own sense of realism.[1]

Scenarios draw on a long history of storytelling. By writing these stories, you will begin to fulfill one of the basic aims of scenario planning, which is to challenge assumptions and facilitate far-sighted strategizing. The scenarios you write will be, as Schwartz[1] mentioned, "a powerful way of avoiding the dangers of denial." The stories can break through denial because they have a narrative quality to them, in that people can picture themselves playing a role in managing the scenario.[2]

Even though you won't focus on strategizing until Step 4, good scenarios will prompt decision-makers to start thinking things like "in this situation we would need to ..." or "to avoid this situation, I would ...." The best way I have found to capture these thoughts without having them derail your scenario development is to note them in the strategies section of a draft report, and revisit them once you have completed all the scenarios. When you get to Step 4 you can review the notes and use those that are still relevant. As was the case with tendencies to strategize according to a single force, strategizing based on a single scenario should be avoided, because it will duplicate efforts required in Step 4, and at this point you would be strategizing to cater only to one rather than multiple plausible futures.

Name the scenarios

Scenario nomenclature is important. Good scenarios have short catchy names that distill their essence. As Wilkinson and Kupers stated, "[a] few words can evoke a world."[5] In story-telling tradition, the name will become jargon for the team developing it, and later the audience, particularly if it connects to a well-known event, fable or legend. For example, "Trojan Horse," "Knight in Shining Armor," "Golden Age," "Armageddon," and "Pinocchio" are all short, well-known names or phrases that convey multifaceted concepts quickly and easily. They also conjure vivid images that are key to bringing each scenario to life, and being remembered. Memorable names will keep the scenario in the minds of decision-makers, and increases the likelihood of them being considered during decision-making.

The names might also be humorous, or carry a theme, and coming up with the name often builds camaraderie in the team. Some of the scenario names used by other scenario planners include those listed below, and although they are in alphabetical order, you will be able to identify at least one set of scenarios named around a playing card theme, and several named after James Bond films, and aircraft:

- Ace of Clubs[19]
- Ace of Diamonds[19]
- Ace of Hearts[19]
- Ace of Spades[19]
- Airbus[20]
- Apocalyptic Transformation[14]
- Balanced Growth[7]
- Beginnings of Sorrow[14]
- Business Class[3, 5]
- Capsize[21]
- Carter Miracle[5]
- Cascading Crises[22]
- Chronic Breakdown[14]
- Concorde[20]
- Confederation Provincialism[23]
- Consolidation[19]
- Convalescence[5]
- Crisis Scenario[5]
- Da Wo[5]
- Defensive Nationalism[23]
- Diamonds are Forever[9, 11]
- Die Another Day[9, 11]
- Dirigiste Solution[5]
- Drift[21]
- European Renaissance[7]
- Focused Growth[23]
- For Your Eyes Only[9, 11]
- Global Crisis[7]
- Global Mercantilism[5]
- Global Shift[7]
- Global Trader[9]
- Global Winner[9]
- Horse and Buggy[20]
- Just Do It![5]
- Living Within Our Means[14]
- Long Boom II[22]
- Mature Calm[14]
- Mountains[5]

- Oceans[5]
- Phantom of the Net[11]
- Portage[21]
- Prism[3, 5]
- Provincial Isolationism[23]
- Regional Player[9]
- Relapse[5]
- Retrenchment[19]
- Safe Refuge[9]
- Shoot the Rapids[21]
- Sustainable World[1, 5]
- The Center Holds[14]
- The Great East-West Match[22]
- The Official Future[1, 14]
- Thunderball[9, 11]
- Titanic[20]
- Uncontrasted Decline[19]
- World of Internal Contradictions[1]

Peter Schwartz[1] suggests that a scenario called "The Official Future" may be a powerful name for a scenario that represents all the assumptions of current strategic planning efforts. Pierre Wack[12] refers to a "surprise-free" scenario that is somewhat similar, in that it challenges assumptions the least. If "The Official Future" is similar to one of your scenarios (perhaps Scenario 2), consider whether the name fits.

Quantify aspects of scenarios where necessary

Your scenarios will likely develop a more qualitative than quantitative nature, because the emphasis of scenario planning is on understanding drivers, their interactions, and their impact on the organization. By viewing each scenario from the perspective of different stakeholders, such as customers, suppliers, the local community, or local policymakers, you can also begin to appreciate that scenarios have enough complexity without trying to quantify them.

However, some aspects may benefit from being quantified, and some audience members will expect some degree of quantification. As you develop your scenarios, quantify those aspects that are possible and make sense, so they can be supported with more than your intuition, collective judgement, and institutional knowledge.

Quantifying aspects of your scenarios will allow you to communicate the organization's exposure to people who will expect to see numbers, like accountants or engineers. As DeAnne Julius, Chief Economist for Shell from 1993 to 1997, was quoted as saying: "Engineers are numbers people, and if you can't quantify what you are talking about, they tend to dismiss you as interesting (at best) mystics."[5] Quantifying relevant aspects of your scenarios will give them more rigor and sophistication.[10] In relation to climate change, the TCFD advised that any organizations "that are likely to be significantly impacted by climate-related transition and/or physical risks should consider some level of quantitative scenario analysis."

It is worthwhile quantifying your scenarios in terms of the organization's and industry's key performance indicators, as well as plausible costs and benefits, to understand what each scenario would mean for the organization. Shell[3] advises using diagrams and tables to show plausible impacts on markets and supply chains. Shell has also used quantitative modeling to ensure scenarios remain plausible.[7]

If quantification is not your forte, then find someone for whom it is. If detailed quantification is out of scope due to expense or other reasons, then do the best you can with your analysis of the driving forces, and develop some quantification skills as you go. Being able to give a ballpark Net Present Value of impacts on asset value, productivity, revenue or costs can be valuable.

Check scenario quality, and abandon or recraft impossible scenarios

As you develop your draft scenarios, you need to critique them to ensure they will tell a persuasive and rigorous story. To be considered plausible, the scenarios need to be internally consistent[1, 6, 8] and have a logical line of reasoning.[5, 8] They must make sense both to the scenario planning team and the intended audience. Ideally, your scenarios will be a combination of plausible and surprising, to break people out of their rational future thinking.

However, while scenario planning surprises us and challenges our assumptions, it does not require us to believe in things that are impossible.[3] Any scenarios that can "be rendered implausible through logical reasoning"[5] and lack internal consistency[7] should be recrafted or abandoned. As Shell[3] has discovered over many years,

> Some aspects of the stories will not work because they are inconsistent with other aspects of the scenarios, irrelevant or too vague; these will need to be discarded or reworked.

Surprise is not a criterion for reworking or discarding a scenario. Nor is likelihood of a scenario emerging.

There are several ways to organize the checking of scenario quality. One way to critique scenarios is to circulate draft scenarios to members of the team for feedback. Another popular method is to roleplay draft scenarios in a workshop, so everyone can consider all the dynamics, stakeholder responses, and impacts.[1]

Once you have rough working drafts of the scenarios to share with the team, you are ready to hold a workshop to check their quality, and develop them further. Box 4.2 outlines a potential workshop agenda.

BOX 4.2 DRAFT SCENARIO ROLEPLAY WORKSHOP

As a structure for the workshop, and in consultation with any facilitator, consider covering the following elements over 1–2 days:

- **Opening:** Introduce the aim and agenda of the workshop: To get feedback on the draft scenarios so they can be prepared for presentation to a broader audience.
- **Review any changes to the scenario framework or scenario baseline** resulting from analysis of the forces and their interactions since the last workshop.
- **Roleplay each draft scenario:** Assign particular decision-maker and stakeholder roles to various team members, and as a team work through each scenario, examining and documenting as many threats, opportunities, and dynamics as can be identified. Rotate the role of main decision-maker among team members as each scenario is discussed to get input from different perspectives about how each scenario could affect the organization and key stakeholders. Ensure you have someone designated as a note-taker to record all the feedback, and make changes to the written scenarios as you go.
- **Conclusion:** To conclude the workshop, summarize what has been achieved – feedback on each draft scenario to facilitate completion, or as far as you got in the process. Provide details of the next workshop.

Through this process, decide whether each scenario should stand as it is, be recrafted (and if so, how), or be abandoned.

Develop new scenarios if necessary

If you have abandoned a scenario, replace it. You might ask, what with? Usually, a team member will have thought about a scenario that falls outside the scope of those produced by the method, perhaps on account of their experience and expertise, and developing that scenario is one option. Another option is to change the presence or extremity of a mid-ranking force (e.g. for LocalBank, extreme weather). A further option is to create a scenario where the state of the economy is different. Whatever scenario you develop, put it through the same development and quality-checking process as the others.

Present draft scenarios for audience feedback

Once you have completed the draft scenarios, they are ready to be presented to a slightly broader executive audience through the next workshop. One practice that you might adopt from Shell[3] is to present the scenarios to a smaller audience of executives before presenting them to progressively wider audiences. This is a good practice. If you present them to executives for feedback first, then work progressively to present to different (perhaps departmental) or more generalized (perhaps whole location or organization) audiences you are bringing everyone along with you, starting at the top to ensure you retain support. This sequence of presentations may also be part of a deliberate presentation roll-out that enables the scenario planning team to gather feedback at each step from a progressively wider range of people.

Presenting the preliminary scenarios to new people provides an opportunity for "fresh eyes" to examine them, but this can also be challenging if some audience members are new to the project. If you frame the event as a workshop to get audience input on the scenarios so far the project can be seen as it truly is: A continuation of earlier interviews and consultation that seeks feedback to help develop solid scenarios and strategies.

Box 4.3 outlines a potential agenda for a workshop.

BOX 4.3 DRAFT SCENARIO AUDIENCE FEEDBACK WORKSHOP

As a structure for the workshop, and in consultation with any facilitator, consider covering the following elements over one day:

- **Opening:** Ask the project champion, the CEO, or similar senior person open the meeting, explain why the project is being undertaken, the audience for and aims of the project, the scope of the project, and highlight their support for it. They can then introduce the project manager, who can (with any facilitator) introduce the aim and agenda of the workshop: To get feedback on the draft scenarios so they can be completed.
- **Provide an overview or review of scenario planning.** This may not be required if everyone in the room knows it already.
- **Provide an overview or review of climate change.** This may not be required if everyone in the room knows it already.
- **State the focal question and time horizon,** and their importance.
- **Review identified key external stakeholders.**
- **Explain the scenario planning method followed,** including identified drivers, ratings, and the final ranking.
- **Review the scenario baseline and scenario framework.**
- **Provide an overview of each draft scenario.**
- **Roleplay each draft scenario:** Assign particular decision-maker and stakeholder roles to various audience members, and as a group work through each scenario, examining the threats, opportunities, and dynamics already identified, and documenting feedback and new insights. Rotate the role of main decision-maker among audience members as each scenario is discussed to get input from different perspectives about how each scenario could affect the organization and key stakeholders.
- **Conclusion:** To conclude the workshop, summarize what has been achieved – feedback on each draft scenario to facilitate completion, or as far as you got in the process.

In this workshop, take time to explain the rationale for the project, the purpose of the scenarios, and the focal question. Without an explanation of the rationale for undertaking scenario planning, you run the risk of the scenarios being less meaningful for your audience, and jeopardizing support for the project. Ask the Chair of the Board or CEO to open the workshop, and to present the rationale for undertaking scenario planning from their point of view. This will give the occasion more weight and legitimacy, and prompt senior key stakeholders to make time to attend. Consider having the Chair of the Board or CEO endorse the scenarios.

Send copies of the scenarios to all audience members well ahead of time, and as Shell[3] suggests, ask them to find their own evidence confirming or refuting each scenario to ensure all discussions remain as evidence-based as possible. Ask your audience to come to the meeting with notes detailing their solutions to each scenario, based on their own knowledge and experience in the organization and industry.

Before you present the scenarios, explain the method used to develop them, including the drivers and driver ranking process. You may also need to explain to your audience the distinction between the focus of scenario planning on uncertainty and impact versus the focus of risk management on probability and impact. Since you are potentially introducing your audience to ideas they will deem radical or unfounded, explaining the drivers behind them is important. Providing them with this book can help you, but if you have veered slightly from what is set out here, explain it.

Another key piece of advice from Shell[3] is to ensure you are not framing the scenarios as predictions, and that your audience is not assuming they are predictions. To avoid the scenarios being perceived as predictions, underscore the dynamics in play within the scenarios, the responses of various stakeholders to them, and the potential implications for the organization. Focusing on these key insights from your work will help everyone to stay on track.

Determine the best order in which to present the scenarios. Lead up to the more confronting scenarios rather than present them first, so your audience does not dismiss them out of surprise, and close you down. In order to influence people you need to keep them onboard, and leading them through less surprising scenarios first is one way to do this.

Avoid assigning probabilities to scenarios[1] (that is, doing risk management), or favoring certain scenarios (that is, letting bias drive the process). Assume the scenarios are all equally probable and that as a set, they present "equally plausible futures."[1] Assigning probabilities or playing favorites undermines the scenario process, because people start focusing on a single scenario which becomes the new rationalized view of the future. Remain open to all scenarios so the organization has the ability to prepare for them all.

Likewise, don't compare the probability of an event in one scenario with another event in a separate scenario, because there is no basis for comparison.[1]

When presenting the scenarios, do so in a way that speaks most directly to your focal question, and think of the advice of Garr Reynolds in his book *Presentation Zen*[24] and incorporate visual and audio content through videos, speech, images, illustrations, and diagrams to convey your message succinctly and convincingly, and help your audience to comprehend your message.

If the scenarios or method challenge the assumptions of anyone in your audience, they may demonstrate signs of discomfort. Part of your workshop introduction should prepare them to feel challenged, and encourage them to speak up when this is the case. Not every member of your audience will agree with or like every scenario or the direction in which the set of scenarios is heading.

Your audience, perhaps like you at the beginning of this process, may not have had a reason to consider futures that differ from what they imagine. It is only natural they may be skeptical of any alternate future you present. It may be important to inform or remind people at this point that the process does not require consensus, but rather embraces and works with different perspectives. As van der Heijden,[8] and Ramírez and Wilkinson[4] wrote, reframing strategic issues occurs more readily in social situations rather than individually, and this is what may be happening in the workshop.

Just as you and your team did when creating the draft scenarios, roleplay each scenario with audience members in the roles of particular decision-makers and stakeholders to engage them in the scenario planning mindset. From their role, they can exert whatever influence that role has over plausible responses to the situation, and they can begin to see the broader picture. This can be an amusing and playful process, but at the same time engages people with the impacts, which can lead to them being more aware of "the assumptions they are making about the world around them."[3]

It is possible that your audience may also suggest moving in new directions, so the scenario planning team may need to emphasize upfront that the team has already put the scenarios through a quality checking process, and the focus of this step is, as Shell[3] notes, "on clarifying the scenarios, rather than adding new ideas," so the scenarios can be completed. Having the project champion or senior decision-maker endorse the scenarios will help address this. Any suggestions to veer from the current path need to be addressed in a way that is not confrontational, which could shut down the discussion, but rather communicates an openness to discovering differences in thinking about the scenarios, or differences in underlying assumptions, which will help to develop the final scenarios.[3]

If your audience highlights inconsistencies or logic flaws in the scenarios, be open to them and work through them together in detail, perhaps through group discussion or focused group work to draw in the views of audience members, and record the outcomes so you can incorporate the feedback into the final scenarios.

Connecting with your audience requires empathy for people who have not been as involved in the project as your team, or may not have been engaged at all. One piece of advice I have given many people to help them self-edit is not to think about what information they want to tell their audience, but to think about what information their audience needs and how they need to receive it. It is your responsibility to ensure the scenarios and any quantitative analysis reach the audience members' priorities and perspectives, not their responsibility to work and make that connection. The scenarios need to incorporate issues about which your audience cares, so you may need to learn about the world view of individual audience members. Here are some final words of wisdom from Shell about presenting your scenarios:

> *There are many ways to communicate scenarios. The simplest method is simply to relate the story of each scenario. However, this still deserves careful thought: storytelling is an art in itself—and oral storytelling demands particular skills. Presenters might find it useful to think about what makes a good spoken narrative—for example, a plot that is easy to follow, the use of suspense and release from suspense, elements of humour, and so on. An important part of communicating scenarios is to connect to the audience's own frame of reference. This is especially true when you are working with global scenarios, where it may be necessary to add locally relevant material. Obviously, in an oral presentation, it is also crucial to employ visual images that work with the narrative, both to capture the attention of the audience and to explain more complex aspects of the story being related. Less obvious is the importance of silence. Pausing will allow the audience to process what they have heard and reflect on how they feel about it. Other methods for vividly communicating a story may include using theatrical or other performance techniques. A short sketch or scene that brings to life a moment in a scenario, although brief, can provide a lucid and compelling snapshot of a scenario story. Using video can offer a storyteller even more creative freedom.*[3]

This step is complete once the draft scenarios have been presented to all key stakeholders, questions have been answered, and feedback has been recorded. Having written feedback directly from your audience or from notes taken at meetings will help you develop the detailed scenarios.

Develop four detailed scenarios

With feedback on your draft scenarios, it is time to develop final scenarios, which will become the foundation for recommendations and strategies. Pierre Wack[6] refers to these scenarios as "decision scenarios," because they will assist decision-making. To decide which feedback should be incorporated into the detailed scenarios, revisit steps you took to create your draft scenarios, and ensure your final scenarios:

a   make sense;
b   answer the focal question;
c   meet the criteria of good scenarios set out in the beginning of this chapter; and are
d   quantified where appropriate and possible.

As you finish the scenarios it becomes even more important to let the priorities of your audience give life to them and not the other way around. As Wack noted, the purpose of scenarios is "to gather and transform information of strategic significance into fresh perceptions."[12] He goes on to mention that the fresh perceptions may not emerge, which is why you need to work hard to appeal to the priorities of your audience, but "[w]hen it works, it is a creative experience that generates a heartfelt 'Aha!' from your managers and leads to strategic insights beyond the mind's previous reach."[12] Presenting the draft scenarios to your audience and receiving feedback on them should have provided clarity about what your final scenarios need to contain to give you the best chance of creating Aha! moments.

Once your detailed scenarios are complete and documented, hold a further team workshop to run through a final check of them, similar to the workshop covered in Box 4.2. Then, you are ready to present the scenarios to an executive audience to start the strategizing process, which is covered in the next chapter.

Given the uncertainties you've identified, it's logical that none of the scenarios you develop will eventuate as envisioned. However, you will have enabled the organization to see that different combinations of drivers, and extreme situations, are plausible, and that preparing for them could save or generate millions of dollars. This is why scenario planning is so powerful – it can help everyone to prepare for the unpredictable and unthinkable. It did not make sense that Hurricane Katrina, or 9/11, or Fukushima happened or had the impacts they did, and yet they continue to affect the world today, and the underlying forces were there for all to see something like them coming at some point.

References

1 Schwartz, P. 1996. *The Art of the Long View: Planning for the Future in an Uncertain World*. New York: Doubleday.
2 Harvard Business School. 2000. Scenario planning reconsidered, *Harvard Management Update*, 5/9: 4.
3 Shell. 2008. *Scenarios: An Explorer's Guide. Exploring the Future*. The Hague: Shell International BV.
4 Ramírez, R. and A. Wilkinson. 2016. *Strategic Reframing: The Oxford Scenario Planning Approach*. Oxford: Oxford University Press.
5 Wilkinson, A. and R. Kupers. 2013. Living in the futures, *Harvard Business Review*, 91/5: 118–127.
6 Wack, P. 1985. Scenarios: Uncharted waters ahead, *Harvard Business Review*, 63/5: 73–89.
7 Schoemaker, P.J.H. 1995. Scenario planning: A tool for strategic thinking, *Sloan Management Review*, 36/2: 25–40.
8 van der Heijden, K. 2005. *Scenarios: The Art of Strategic Conversation*. 2nd edn. Chichester, UK: John Wiley & Sons.
9 Wade, W. 2012. *Scenario Planning: A Field Guide to the Future*. Hoboken, USA: John Wiley & Sons.
10 TCFD. 2016. *The Use of Scenario Analysis in Disclosure of Climate-Related Risks and Opportunities*. Financial Stability Board Task Force on Climate-Related Financial Disclosures. https://www.fsb-tcfd.org/publications/technical-supplement/#, accessed 20 Feb 2017.
11 Lindgren, M. and H. Bandhold. 2009. *Scenario Planning: The Link Between Future and Strategy*. 2nd edn. Houndmills, UK: Palgrave Macmillan.
12 Wack, P. 1985. Scenarios: Shooting the rapids, *Harvard Business Review*, 63/6: 139–150.

13 Schoemaker, P.J.H. 1998. Twenty common pitfalls in scenario planning, in *Learning from the Future: Competitive Foresight Scenarios*, ed. L. Fahey and R.M. Randall. New York: John Wiley & Sons. pp. 422–431.

14 Hawken, P., J. Ogilvy and P. Schwartz. 1982. *Seven Tomorrows: Toward a Voluntary History*. Covelo, CA: Bantam Books.

15 Porter, M.E. 1979. How competitive forces shape strategy, *Harvard Business Review*, 57/2: 137–145.

16 Schoemaker, P.J.H. 1997. Disciplined imagination: From scenarios to strategic options, *International Studies of Management & Organization*, 27/2: 43–70.

17 Hitt, M.A., R.D. Ireland and R.E. Hoskisson. 2014. *Strategic Management: Competitiveness and Globalization*. 11th edn. Stamford, CT: Cengage Learning.

18 Leonard-Barton, D. 1992. Core capabilities and core rigidities: A paradox in managing new product development, *Strategic Management Journal*, 13: 111.

19 Martelli, A. 2014. *Models of Scenario Building and Planning: Facing Uncertainty and Complexity*. Bocconi on Management, ed. R. Grant. Houndmills, UK: Palgrave Macmillan.

20 Chermack, T.J. 2011. *Scenario Planning in Organizations: How to Create, Use, and Assess Scenarios*. Oakland, CA: Berrett-Koehler.

21 Kahane, A. 2012. *Transformative Scenario Planning: Working Together to Change the Future*. San Francisco: Berrett-Koehler.

22 Schwartz, P. 2011. *Learnings from the Long View*. Global Business Network.

23 Ralston, B. and I. Wilson. 2006. *The Scenario-Planning Handbook: A Practitioner's Guide to Developing and Using Scenarios to Direct Strategy in Today's Uncertain Times*. Mason, OH: Thomson/South-Western.

24 Reynolds, G. 2011. *Presentation Zen: Simple Ideas on Presentation Design and Delivery*. Berkeley, CA: New Riders.

5

STEP 4: IDENTIFY WARNING SIGNALS, STRATEGIZE, AND ASSESS

The aim of scenario planning is to develop strategies,[1] or recommendations for those responsible for developing strategies.[2] This chapter will help you to answer the second and third parts of your focal question: "… what should we do, and when?" By compelling us to think about plausible scenarios, and considering the potential timing and content of responses, scenario planning reduces exposure to whatever will eventuate. In this final step of the method, you will identify warning signals to monitor so your organization can anticipate what future could be unfolding as time progresses, and develop broad strategies or recommendations to prepare. You will also assess the project to understand its effectiveness and improve the process for next time.

Identify warning signals

Any scenario you have developed could plausibly emerge as time progresses, but it's unlikely to emerge exactly as envisioned, because the rest of the world surrounding it also continues to evolve. To know which future is unfolding, and how, you need to identify and monitor warning signals that indicate potential scenario activity. As Antonio Martelli mentioned in his book *Models of Scenario Building and Planning: Facing Uncertainty and Complexity*, "useful (i.e. usable) signals are those containing information that portends change."[3] Warning signals indicate which future is emerging,[4] and indicate junctions and turning points along the way.[3] By monitoring them regularly, you will keep your strategic decision-making ahead of threats and opportunities, and ahead of competitors.

To identify warning signals, start by discussing each driver and scenario and the trends and events important to them. You may need to revisit research done to rate the drivers and develop the scenarios, so you can detect warning signals that are important to various parts of the organization. This process may also be another point at which organizational assumptions about the future are unearthed.[5]

Invest equal effort to identify and monitor both strong signals and "weak signals"[3, 6] as Schoemaker and Martelli call them. Weak signals are those that are more subtle,[4] and will help you identify trends that are still out of sight to the untrained eye. Do not confuse weak signals with unimportant signals: A weak signal may present as obscure, imprecise, or indistinct news, but might grow to become significant,[3] and perhaps even become a driving force in its own right. It is in the identification and monitoring of weak signals that you can gain most insight about what future will emerge.

Identify warning signals from drivers

The drivers are an obvious place to start looking for warning signals, since they may already be apparent. Examine the drivers to isolate warning signals to monitor. Warning signals may be trends, events, tipping points, changes in dynamics, or other things the team believes need to be tracked. Some warning signals may be tracked using a spreadsheet, while others could be mapped to create a visual record, or recorded like an oral or written history of qualitative anecdotal evidence. Examples of warning signals and events that might be important to the hypothetical LocalBank could include:

- Precipitation (rain and snowfall) levels in the greater Boston area, tracking measures such as average monthly and seasonal precipitation levels, and recording any flooding events;
- The implementation or cancellation of federal, state, or city infrastructure projects in the greater Boston area, detailing type, purpose, location, progress, and other relevant details;
- Extreme weather events directly or indirectly affecting the greater Boston area, tracking such details as their type, location, timing, severity, and resulting damage or insurance losses;
- Ambient temperature over land in the greater Boston area, tracking measures such as average monthly and seasonal temperature, and recording specific events, such as heatwaves or cold snaps;
- Sea level change in the greater Boston area, tracking average highest high tides and lowest low tides over a given period, and recording the levels and any coastal or inland flooding during specific events, such as king tides or extreme weather events;
- Ocean temperature in the ocean off the coast of Boston and New England, tracking such things as average monthly and seasonal temperature, and recording specific temperatures at the time of extreme weather events;
- Anecdotes of residents living in properties for whom LocalBank holds mortgages;
- Responses to any of the above by key stakeholders, such as customers, suppliers, and policymakers.

Beyond the above potential warning signals, LocalBank might also decide it's useful to go deeper. Taking sea level change as an example: LocalBank could also monitor updates to flood maps, property re-zoning, or do research of its own to determine how other businesses in its area have been affected by rising sea levels, how they have responded or are planning to respond.

Identify warning signals from scenarios

Next, look for warning signals in your scenarios. As Shell learned, "[e]vents in the world may 'signal' that the dynamics of a particular scenario are actually developing."[5] What interactions between drivers, or specific events might indicate that a particular scenario is emerging? Place yourself in each scenario and ask, "What trends or events would forewarn us of this scenario's emergence?" As you do this for each scenario, you may find bellwethers that indicate the direction in which the future is heading. Warning signals may be directly or indirectly related to a given scenario, or may provide some indication that the broader context is changing. They will also help you identify if there is a shift occurring from one unfolding scenario to another, or if new drivers or dynamics are emerging.

For LocalBank, scenario-related drivers could include the following:

- Passing of a particular infrastructure funding bill at national, state, or city levels, or initiation of a significant infrastructure project in the greater Boston area;
- Infrastructure technology and building material trends, and the development of a particular type of technology or building material;
- The development or redevelopment of standards surrounding a particular type of infrastructure;
- The appointment or election of a particular person to important positions of power;
- The state of the Massachusetts and U.S. economy; and
- Population growth or decline in the greater Boston area, by suburb.

For each warning signal identified from drivers and scenarios, consider how it can be monitored, directly measured if necessary, by who and how often, and set up a system for recording and monitoring. Monitoring the warning signals is a long-term commitment, and is one way that members of the scenario planning team and the broader organization can stay connected to the ongoing scenario planning effort.

By monitoring each warning signal, you will get to know what changes are happening and when, and this will inform what action may be required, and when, which will help to develop the important capability of strategic timing.

Develop strategies or recommendations

The transition to developing strategies or recommendations can feel like the point you've been waiting for all along, especially because at several junctions in the method I advised you to wait until you had worked through all the previous steps before doing substantive work on this step. Hopefully you can see the value in waiting, because you are now in a position to develop strategic options based on a solid foundation of research and scenarios that have given the team a holistic understanding of how climate change might affect the organization.

As with the previous step, this one should draw in team members and key members of your audience. Box 5.1 outlines a potential workshop agenda to begin developing strategic options. If your scenario planning project is developing strategies rather than recommendations, consider whether it makes sense for the workshop to run as preparation for the scenarios to be integrated into the next scheduled round of general strategic planning. Complementing the organization's existing strategic planning process with scenario planning will be a significant step towards better long-term and short-term strategic management. It will also ensure strategic options are properly evaluated and costed, and that appropriate executive or Board support is gained. As Lindgren and Bandhold[7] mentioned:

> *If scenario planning is not simply to be a pleasant exercise, someone in the organization must be responsible for continuity, and one or more people for drawing conclusions from the exercise and working out its consequences for the choice of strategies …*

Incorporating scenario planning into the strategic management process is the best way to ensure scenario planning is not simply a toothless exercise.

BOX 5.1 STRATEGY DEVELOPMENT WORKSHOP

As a structure for the workshop, and in consultation with any facilitator, consider covering the following elements over 1–2 days:

- **Opening:** Introduce the aim and agenda of the workshop: Review scenarios and warning signals, and begin developing strategies or recommendations.
- **Review scenarios and their impacts**, focusing on the question "How would the scenarios affect the organization?" and in particular looking for common impacts among the scenarios. See further details in this chapter.
- **Review warning signals**, and facilitate discussion about others that might be appropriate.
- **Review current strategies**, answering the question "How do our current strategies, policies and capabilities prepare the organization for the scenarios?" See further details in this chapter.
- **Begin developing strategic options**, prompted by the questions "What new strategic options should be considered now and the future?" and "For strategies to be implemented in future, what warning signals would trigger their implementation?" See further details in this chapter. This can be done as a whole group, or with break-out groups focusing on different impacts, business units, locations, or other foci. Consider role-playing strategies as you may have done with scenarios.

- **Conclusion:** To conclude the workshop, summarize what has been achieved – the development of draft strategic options, or as far as you got in the process.

How would the scenarios affect the organization?

You already know the answer to this question in relation to each separate scenario, but answering this question requires you to identify the impacts that are common to multiple scenarios. This analysis can begin with examining the impacts brought by your scenario baseline, which is common to all your scenarios, and then move on to those aspects that make each scenario unique. Perhaps multiple scenarios could leave the organization exposed to such things as changes in cash reserves or key investments, damage to infrastructure, asset depreciation, loss of water or energy supply, changes in key supplies or markets. Alternatively, consider whether multiple scenarios might expand a market, cause assets to appreciate, bring product development opportunities, or reduce costs.

For LocalBank, all the scenarios include a scenario baseline of sea level rise and extreme weather events, both of which could devalue some properties in its mortgage portfolio, while causing others to appreciate. On top of this, two scenarios include increased precipitation change, which could increase inland flooding and further affecting property values. The scenarios may also highlight and exacerbate existing vulnerabilities that are not climate-specific, such as over-reliance on one key supplier or customer: In LocalBank's case, this vulnerability could be over-reliance on one small geographic area (Greater Boston).

How do our current strategies, policies, and capabilities prepare the organization for the scenarios?

Scenario planning allows decision-makers to review current strategies, policies, and capabilities with fresh and more critical eyes, which should lead to the re-evaluation of current strategies. Consider mapping the organization's current strategies, policies, and capabilities onto the three basic levels of strategy:

- Corporate strategy, which answers the question of what industry/ies should we be competing in?[8] Which industry/ies is your organization in? LocalBank is in the banking industry, and competes in the local market of that industry.
- Business strategy, which answers the question of how should our business/es compete in its industry/ies?[8] How does your organization compete? How does your organization differentiate itself from its competitors? Even if your organization is non-profit, you are still operating in an industry, and likely competing for funding. As a local bank, LocalBank differentiates itself from its competitors based on more personalized customer service through suburban branches, and products developed with the needs of local customers in mind.

It is not necessarily cheaper or offering better rates than its competitors. LocalBank aims to grow by a mixture of organic expansion and expansion by acquisition, and by developing new savings and loan products.

- Functional strategy, which answers the question of how does each part of the organization support the business strategy? Any analysis you've done about the organization's capabilities can help you determine how each function or department contributes to the business strategy. How do the sales, marketing, business development, customer service, human resources, research and development, purchasing, information technology, government relations, or other parts of the organization work in ways that support the business strategy? It is at this level that policies are often written. For LocalBank, this would include customer service, business development, human resources, risk management, finance, compliance, and other functional areas.

By examining current strategies through the lens of your scenarios, their impacts, and the projected state of warning signals, you will start to understand which current strategies might remain robust, and which need to be reconsidered.

In addition, written and unwritten policies that determine an organization's ability to respond to the scenarios may need to be considered. For instance, if purchasing policies dictate only ordering from suppliers of a particular type, in a particular location, or affiliated with a particular organization or program, then this may influence an organization's ability to respond. Van der Heijden mentioned that "scenarios are the testbed through which an area of policy is considered and judged."[1] Given the organization has little to no influence over the climate change scenarios you have developed, compromise may need to come from within, including policies.

Further to strategies and policies, seeing the scenarios laid out will also enable you to examine the "degree of fit between the organization's core capabilities and the variety of plausible future conditions," as Wilkinson and Kupers advocated.[9] Your organization may already have capabilities that could become a strength when responding to particular scenarios, and other areas where capabilities are lacking that would leave the organization exposed. Both capabilities and lack of them are good starting points for strategizing.[7]

Once the scenario planning team understands the degree to which current strategies, policies and capabilities are preparing it for the scenarios (especially the scenario baseline), consider ways they might feasibly be updated so the organization can respond effectively to newly identified certainties, uncertainties, risks, and opportunities.

What new strategic options should be considered now and the future?

You've probably already started to think of new strategic options, since earlier steps of the method prompted these considerations. To begin answering the above question, consider that the more scenarios in which a particular positive or negative impact appears, the more likely the organization will experience it regardless of what future unfolds. If an impact appears in only one scenario, then immediately implementing a strategy for it could be high-risk – what Schwartz[4] calls a "bet-the-company strategy," or at least create unnecessary costs. However, when impacts appear across multiple scenarios (such as those associated with your scenario baseline), the organization may need some kind of strategy regardless of what future unfolds. Shell put it this way:

> *It may be that for certain aspects of your business, whichever scenario might occur, whatever events the future may hold, the implications of a particular strategy seem certain to remain the same. This may suggest to decision makers that there is a set of actions that they can—perhaps, should—implement fairly immediately and securely. The decision to move on other strategic options, however, will be contingent on how they play out in the different scenarios, and that, of course, depends on which way the external environment actually develops.[5]*

Aside from strategies responding to impacts occurring in multiple scenarios, there may be other "no regrets" strategies that it makes sense to implement regardless of what future unfolds. Circles of Climate[10] has developed a *No Regrets Charter* for how cities should respond to climate change, which provides a useful definition of no regrets strategies for climate change that organizations can easily interpret for themselves:

> *No Regrets strategies are based on concepts and measures that can begin to be enacted now without being certain about all dimensions of future climate change. Measures are taken and strategies are thus adopted in a precautionary sense with the aim of responding to possible negative impacts before they intensify. Such measures are advisable for future generations, but also relevant to enhancing the living conditions of people in the present.*
>
> *No Regrets strategies crosses the boundary between adaptation and mitigation. With No Regrets strategies, the benefits of adaptation and mitigation measures therefore continue even if the effects of climate change are not as horrific as currently anticipated.[10]*

Impacts that appear salient regardless of the scenario, and where no regrets strategies make sense, can produce a range of immediate and delayed strategic options that might include things such as the following, which the TCFD suggests: Investing in new capabilities, adjusting financial arrangements, altering the investment portfolio, investing in new technologies, or updating the business model.[11] Also consider adding partnerships to this list, since building resilience requires coordination between organizations, communities in which they operate, infrastructure providers, policymakers, and others. Finally, add to the list the potential need to relocate capital assets in response to extreme changes in local conditions.

Develop a list of strategic options or recommendations within the three levels of strategy that might be implemented now or in future:

- Corporate strategy: What do your scenarios broadly indicate about the potential future state of your industry/ies? Could it become less or more profitable in future, or remain about the same? Changing industry or sector is a big move, but if new corporate strategies are potentially necessary in future, it's worthwhile considering it now rather than later.
- Business strategy: What do your scenarios indicate about the potential future nature of competition within your current or new industry/ies? What new business strategies, or changes to existing strategies, might enable it to remain competitive in future?
- Functional strategy: What do your scenarios tell you about what new capabilities, or changes to existing capabilities, may be needed in various parts of your organization to support the business strategy? Do the scenarios suggest whether existing or new capabilities should be developed in-house or outsourced in future?

In LocalBank's case, in response to the presence of a number of drivers relating to flooding – infrastructure adaptation, precipitation, sea level change, and extreme weather – broad strategic options could include functional tactics like implementing a policy to check local flood maps before finance is granted for a property, or before a new branch is located, and working with customers to adapt properties already subject to mortgages, to business strategies like relocating existing branches or enhancing its online presence to ensure it can continue to meet customers' needs while not exposing branches to something like sea level rise. The timing of any of these will depend on the current and projected states of warning signals.

For strategies to be implemented in future, what warning signals would trigger their implementation?

Scenario planning comes into its full power when considering the potential timing of responses to plausible but uncertain futures. Some strategic options may not need to be implemented for years or even for decades, but developing the options now enables the organization to consider at what point in future it might need to implement a specific course of action, and what would trigger it. Taking the time now to determine the timing of strategies allows you to do it while you have more time, more flexibility, and more objectivity.

A tool that Shell[5] uses, and an idea I borrow, is to develop a timeline on which past and potential future events can be plotted. Plotting past events can help everyone understand the organization's responses to them, and plotting potential future events, including future potential states of warning signals, will help to visualize what is possible, and the points at which action might be needed.

Since there are no guarantees about whether and when a scenario might occur, consider developing strategic options that have inbuilt timing flexibility. Wack noted that managers he worked with developed different strategic options depending on where in the business cycle a particular scenario occurred.[12] What cycles influence your organization? The general economic cycle? A seasonal cycle? Something else? If your organization is non-profit, funding and grant-making cycles may also be important.

As you develop strategic options and their potential timing, think about how key partners, suppliers, and customers might respond given the potential situation at that point. Workshop participants might roleplay strategic options keeping in mind specific clients,[5] suppliers, or community stakeholders, especially if they need to be onboard for a given option to succeed.

Something else that will help you discern the feasibility of each option is considering whether potential trade-offs exist in the strategic options, and how they can be managed. This is an important consideration put forward by Martina Linnenluecke and Andrew Griffiths, in their book, *The Climate Resilient Organization: Adaptation and Resilience to Climate Change and Weather Extremes.*[13] Perhaps the most obvious trade-off will surround the cost of any strategic option, but there may also be other trade-offs, between climate change mitigation and adaptation initiatives, such as adaptation strategies that would increase carbon emissions, or mitigation strategies that would expose the organization to other climate vulnerabilities. Consider which trade-offs are worth making, and why. Aim to create synergies where possible, such as a strategic option that reduces carbon emissions, increases adaptation efforts, and improves the bottom line.

Beyond this, Linnenluecke and Griffiths[13] also raise an important question of whether climate change impacts might push an organization beyond its ability to adapt. We have little understanding about the limits of organizational adaptation to climate change, because innovations such as irrigation and genetic modification technologies have helped us in the past to work beyond physical and ecological limits. When might it become impossible for your organization to adapt, and what strategic options should be developed to manage the situation proactively?

Once the team has worked their way through these discussions, you will have a list of strategic options that will evolve as team members take them back to their parts of the organization for consideration and refinement. Once the list of strategic options is somewhat firm, and their timing has been considered, cost them as much as you are able. This will give you a better idea of their feasibility, and will indicate the degree to which they need to be endorsed by executives and the Board.

The process of developing recommendations or strategic options and their timing is an iterative one that should eventually arrive at a point where you have a firm set of options and agreement about what should be implemented now, what may need to be implemented in future, and what could trigger their implementation.

Communicate strategies or recommendations

Just as you did when presenting your scenarios, it's important to get feedback on the draft strategic options from senior stakeholders. To do this, Box 5.2 outlines a potential agenda for a strategy feedback workshop.

BOX 5.2 STRATEGY FEEDBACK WORKSHOP

As a structure for the workshop, and in consultation with any facilitator, consider covering the following elements over half to one day:

- **Opening:** Ask the project champion, the CEO, or similar senior person open the meeting, and endorse the project's progress, before the project manager or facilitator introduces the aim and agenda of the workshop: To present draft strategies or recommendations for feedback.
- **Review and discuss common impacts identified among the scenarios.**
- **Review and discuss the warning signals to be tracked.**
- **Review and discuss current strategies:** Present and discuss results of work determining the efficacy of current strategies, policies, and capabilities, and any recommendations to update them; taking onboard feedback.
- **Present and discuss recommendations and strategies** resulting from work answering the question "What new strategic options should be considered now and in the future?" Consider role-playing strategies with your audience, taking into account how key customers, suppliers, partners, and competitors might respond, as you may have done with scenarios, and take onboard feedback.
- **Conclusion:** Summarize what has been achieved – receiving feedback on each recommendation or strategy, or as far as you got in the process.

Similar to developing the final scenarios, take onboard feedback from this workshop to develop a final set of strategic options or recommendations. When you are ready, take a similar approach to when you developed and presented your scenarios by presenting your final strategic options to a progressively wider audience once they have been approved for their consumption. Tailor your presentation to each audience, even if it's a general presentation. Shell[5] takes this approach to ensure the presentation is engaging for every audience and for every member of every audience, so the scenarios remain relevant and impactful.

When should we redo our scenario planning?

Scenario planning works best when done "iteratively, as opposed to being a one-off project" so it can keep facilitating organizational learning.[14] Shell observed that its 20-year scenarios tend to remain useful for 3–4 years, then they need to be redone.[5] The new knowledge you've created is a powerful and valuable asset that needs to be maintained as such, and like most strategies, the results of scenario planning have a "limited shelf life" as they become familiar and start to constrain thinking.[9]

If not already integrated, scenario planning will work best when it is integrated into the existing strategic planning cycle, so it can continue to add value to the five-year traditional strategic plan and be repeated at appropriate intervals (or when needed). This way, you will continually learn what you need to know to support rigorous strategic decision-making. Annual updates of scenarios have been per-formed by some companies during turbulent times,[15] while every 3–5 years might suffice in calmer times.

Another reason for repeating the scenario planning process regularly, and within the strategic planning process, is that you may not get everything right each time. Even Peter Schwartz, who is arguably the most famous scenario planner, gets it wrong occasionally. In his book *Learnings from the Long View*,[16] Schwartz listed what he called four bad calls, three success stories and lessons learned since he published *The Art of the Long* View;[4] the point being that you may catch things the next time around.

To ensure the relevance of your next scenario planning project, experienced scenario planners advise starting from the beginning,[5, 9] rather than assuming the existing scenarios will still be relevant. Developing new scenarios will help to counter any tendency to "cling to" existing scenarios,[9] while also appreciating and adding to work done in the present round.[5] This may mean the process is led by a new team leader and some new team members to bring new approaches and ideas[9] to continue to build scenario planning capabilities within the organization.

You are almost finished, except for scheduling the next round of scenario planning, and assessing the project.

Assess the scenario planning project

You might be asking why assessment is not included as a separate step in the sce-nario planning method, rather than being included in the final step. It's so it is done, and not treated as an optional extra. This is also why I suggested in Chapter 2 that you read this section ahead of starting the project. Scenario planning projects need to be assessed, to get the most out of them, to understand their effectiveness, and to improve the process for next time.

In his book *Scenario Planning in Organizations*,[17] Thomas Chermack added valuable insights about assessing the results of scenario planning. Chermack mentioned that it can be difficult to assess some aspects of scenario planning projects. Others, such as Adam Kahane have also cited the difficulty "of not really knowing whether the pro-cesses have produced failure or success," because they are not direct or immediate.[18] Assessing scenario planning may seem difficult, but I would counter that it's no more or less difficult than assessing the results of other strategic planning processes.

Chermack's work covering assessment was based on earlier work by Swanson and Holton,[19] which proposed evaluating satisfaction, learning, and performance in the assessment of any organizational intervention. Below, I briefly describe Swan-son and Holton's framework, as applied by Chermack to scenario planning, and apply it here to scenario planning for climate change.

Assess satisfaction

Satisfaction assessment examines the degree to which project participants and key stakeholders were satisfied with the scenario planning project.[17, 19] There are various ways to capture this information, such as by asking your team and key stakeholders to complete a questionnaire, interviewing them, or conducting focus groups. Chermack's assessment asks participants to rate their agreement with statements such as "I have a better understanding of challenges facing the organization" and "This project has possible long-term benefits for the organization," as well as asking them open-ended questions about the most and least valuable parts of the project.[17] I recommend using Chermack's satisfaction survey,[17] which also measures learning to some degree, or developing your own. See the reference list for details of Chermack's book.[17] If you opt for interviews or focus groups, develop a set of open-ended questions that include broad questions about what were the most and least valuable aspects of the project. Have someone take detailed notes, or record the sessions if feasible.

In addition to reporting the quantitative results from any questionnaire, also look for themes in qualitative feedback, where multiple people have made the same or similar statements, and use this feedback to recommend improvements for the next round of scenario planning.

Assess learning

Learning assessment records the knowledge and expertise that participants and key stakeholders gained through the project; what they "know and can do differently as a result of their engagement in the project."[17] Chermack[17] provides a detailed approach to assessing learning, including information about various assessment tools that are available. Chermack provides a questionnaire that team members and key stakeholders might take before the project to provide a baseline, and again after the project to assess learning compared to that baseline. Scenario planning projects being done within larger companies might benefit from taking Chermack's pre-test/post-test approach to learning assessment, or developing their own; however, smaller companies might simply rely on the questions within the satisfaction survey noted above. Below are a few questions inspired by those suggested by Chermack, and tailored for climate change:

- What did you learn about the organization in relation to climate change by being involved in the scenario planning project?
- How (if at all) has what you learned altered the way you consider climate change in making decisions?
- What (if any) were the key insights you gained about the organization in relation to climate change?
- How (if at all) do you work differently as a result of what you learned about climate change and the organization?
- How (if at all) do you observe others working differently, perhaps as a result of what they learned about the organization and climate change?

Again, look for themes in qualitative feedback, where multiple people have made similar statements, and use this feedback to make recommendations to improve the project next time.

Assess performance

Performance assessment may include general *system* measures, such as outputs or efficiency measures, and *financial* measures, such as revenue, profit, or costs (including project costs).[17, 19] Many of these measures will already exist and can be tracked before and after the project. You may also develop new measures after the project. For instance, LocalBank could begin to measure the percentage of its loans that are exposed to significant impacts of climate change, and the value of its property portfolio in affected areas.

System and financial performance may be continually monitored before and long after the project. Once you have initial measurements, add them to project documentation, along with any changes, especially those that may be attributable to the project, and use them to recommend improvements for the next round of scenario planning. You may also be able to identify ways in which the project could be run more cost-efficiently next time.

Once you have the results from assessing satisfaction, learning, and performance, hold a final project team meeting to present them and complete the set of recommendations for next time.

Congratulations, you have reached the end of the method! By working your way through the method, which has forced you to think about uncomfortable things including your worst case scenario, you have developed strategic options that will help the organization manage whatever future ultimately unfolds. This is no small feat, and you and your team should feel the sense of accomplishment. It is a significant thing you have done. If you have followed the method, you should understand the sense of freedom, calm, and resilience that comes from knowing and preparing for a variety of futures. The next concluding chapter will provide some time to reflect on the whole process.

References

1 van der Heijden, K. 2005. *Scenarios: The Art of Strategic Conversation.* 2nd edn. Chichester, UK: John Wiley & Sons.

2 Ralston, B. and I. Wilson. 2006. *The Scenario-Planning Handbook: A Practitioner's Guide to Developing and Using Scenarios to Direct Strategy in Today's Uncertain Times.* Mason, OH: Thomson/South-Western.

3 Martelli, A. 2014. *Models of Scenario Building and Planning: Facing Uncertainty and Complexity.* Bocconi on Management, ed. R. Grant. Houndmills, UK: Palgrave Macmillan.

4 Schwartz, P. 1996. *The Art of the Long View: Planning for the Future in an Uncertain World.* New York: Doubleday.

5 Shell. 2008. *Scenarios: An Explorer's Guide. Exploring the Future.* The Hague: Shell International BV.

6 Schoemaker, P.J.H. 1995. Scenario planning: A tool for strategic thinking, *Sloan Management Review*, 36/2: 25–40.

7 Lindgren, M. and H. Bandhold. 2009. *Scenario Planning: The Link Between Future and Strategy.* 2nd edn. Houndmills, UK: Palgrave Macmillan.

8 Hitt, M.A., R.D. Ireland and R.E. Hoskisson. 2014. *Strategic Management: Competitiveness and Globalization*. 11th edn. Stamford, CT: Cengage Learning.

9 Wilkinson, A. and R. Kupers. 2013. Living in the futures, *Harvard Business Review*, 91/5: 118–127.

10 circlesofclimate.org. 2018. The Meaning of a No Regrets Strategy. http://www.circle sofclimate.org/, accessed 11 March 2018.

11 TCFD. 2016. *The Use of Scenario Analysis in Disclosure of Climate-Related Risks and Opportunities*. Financial Stability Board Task Force on Climate-Related Financial Disclosures. https://www.fsb-tcfd.org/publications/technical-supplement/#, accessed 20 Feb 2017.

12 Wack, P. 1985. Scenarios: Uncharted waters ahead, *Harvard Business Review*, 63/5: 73–89.

13 Linnenluecke, M.K. and A. Griffiths. 2015. *The Climate Resilient Organization: Adaptation and Resilience to Climate Change and Weather Extremes*. Cheltenham, UK: Edward Elgar.

14 Ramírez, R. and A. Wilkinson. 2016. *Strategic Reframing: The Oxford Scenario Planning Approach*. Oxford: Oxford University Press.

15 Wack, P. 1985. Scenarios: Shooting the rapids, *Harvard Business Review*, 63/6: 139–150.

16 Schwartz, P. 2011. *Learnings from the Long View*. Global Business Network.

17 Chermack, T.J. 2011. *Scenario Planning in Organizations: How to Create, Use, and Assess Scenarios*. Oakland, CA: Berrett-Koehler.

18 Kahane, A. 2012. *Transformative Scenario Planning: Working Together to Change the Future*. San Francisco: Berrett-Koehler.

19 Swanson, R.A. and E.F. Holton. 1999. *Results: How to Assess Performance, Learning and Perceptions in Organizations*. San Francisco: Berret-Koehler.

CONCLUSION

In their scenario work, both Schwartz[1] and van der Heijden[2] underscored the usefulness of scenario planning not only for considering alternate futures, but also as a basis for having "strategic conversations" that foster constant organizational learning and strategic flexibility in the face of changing markets, changing operating environments, and a changing climatic environment. Reaching the end of the scenario planning method can mark the advancement towards a broader, holistic strategic planning method, where the five-year rolling strategic plan can be developed within the context of long-term drivers and dynamics, including those associated with climate change.

Scenario planning is both a readily applicable and scalable approach to planning and strategizing. It is readily applicable, because it can be applied to a wide range of long-term questions. Here you have applied it to climate change, but now that you understand the method and its dynamics, you can apply it to any strategizing or planning. The method was developed for broad strategizing that helps organizations tackle the bigger picture questions that include competitors, regulators, markets, suppliers, partners, the business cycle, and it would be a waste not to use this newly developed asset to address other issues facing your organization. It is also a method that is scalable, since it can be, and has been, useful at many different levels. Here, it has been applied at the organization level, but applying it to a partnership, a surrounding community or a city, a geographic area, a market, or any other analytical level is also possible, and likely useful.

Scenario planning should also have helped you to develop a long-term sense of timing for your organization about climate change. This can also apply to other short and long-term strategic issues, as you recognize when to start investing time and money in a certain direction, or stop investing in another, and to rethink policies that underpin strategic decision-making.

However, be prepared not to get real traction until you get a first success at anticipating a threat or opportunity coming over the horizon. Many people, especially the skeptics you encountered along the way, need a concrete and tangible foreseen event to give them confidence in the scenario method. As Pierre Wack noted about his work with Shell,[3] once people can see a threat that has been averted or an opportunity seized they may quickly convert.

Has the method helped to avoid strategizing based on past results for a single vision of the future? If you have followed the method, you have now imagined four plausible futures, and you have also developed strategic options to respond to them. Something Kees van der Heijden[2] said in concluding his book *Scenarios: The Art of the Strategic Conversation*, is that "[i]f there is one element essential to success it is being able to develop new and unique insights about the world. Without this no strategy can succeed." You and others in your organization will by now have built skills that do not rely on, and are cautious of, a single vision of the future, because you now know how to develop strategies that develop unique insights about the world, and that embrace and prepare for the uncertainties of multiple plausible futures. Past results are now only of historical contextual interest.

Is this enough to overcome optimism bias? Or, will it persist in the wake of having worked through the scenario planning method? After all, Tali Sharot's work has found that people downplay the likelihood of them experiencing a negative scenario.[4] Merely knowing about optimism bias and following the scenario planning method to develop a range of scenarios may not be enough. My hope is that the method set out in this book has facilitated enough thought about what action is required, and when, to help to manage optimism bias, overcome optimism-based inertia, and promote you and your organization to a position of increased climate and strategic resilience.

In addition to repeating your scenario planning efforts, and integrating them into your strategic planning process, consider, as Wack[3] did, informing governments or industry associations of what your organization sees advancing over the horizon, and relating it to indicators and worldviews that matter to them. If this is an option, note his advice of tailoring the delivery to each audience specifically, and ensuring include things that are of concern to each type of audience member. Wilkinson and Kupers[5] also noted that scenarios can be leveraged to "add color to corporate speeches, to open doors to privileged conversations with resource holders and governments, and to build a network of NGO contacts."

I wish you well on your journey towards organizational resilience in the face of climate change.

References

1 Schwartz, P. 1996. *The Art of the Long View: Planning for the Future in an Uncertain World*. New York: Doubleday.

2 van der Heijden, K. 2005. *Scenarios: The Art of Strategic Conversation*. 2nd edn. Chichester, UK: John Wiley & Sons.
3 Wack, P. 1985. Scenarios: Uncharted waters ahead, *Harvard Business Review*, 63/5: 73–89.
4 Sharot, T., A.M. Riccardi, C.M. Raio and E.A. Phelps. 2007. Neural mechanisms mediating optimism bias, *Nature*, 450/7166: 102–105.
5 Wilkinson, A. and R. Kupers. 2013. Living in the futures, *Harvard Business Review*, 91/5: 118–127.

CLIMATE DRIVER SUMMARIES

To help with your initial identification of climate change drivers potentially affecting your organization, summaries for a sample of 12 known climate-change-related trends are included in the following pages. The drivers cover each STEEP analysis category: Social, Technological, Economic, Ecological, and Political/Legal. For each driver summary, there is a description of the driver, as well as examples of how it is affecting organizations now, and how it may affect organizations in 25 years' time. Since these drivers may become outdated as climate science, society, policy, and other things progress, you should think of the summaries as being useful for initial brainstorming, while doing additional research to ensure you are identifying drivers that are specific to your organization. The drivers covered in this Appendix are:

- Social

    a   Societal understanding of and debate about climate change
    b   Socially responsible investing and activist investors

- Technological

    a   Renewable energy and energy efficient technologies
    b   Water-efficient technologies

- Economic

    a   Climate-related competition
    b   Public–Private Partnerships

- Ecological

    a   Sea level change
    b   Rising temperature

c   Changes in precipitation (including drought)
d   Extreme weather

• Political/Legal

a   International climate change policy
b   Water policy

More climate driver summaries are available at www.nardiahaigh.com.

Social drivers

Societal understanding of and debate about climate change

Overview

In 2002, political consultant Frank Luntz crafted a memo explaining that as long as "voters believe there is no consensus about global warming within the scientific community," environmental regulation would stall.[1] In 2012, Kelly Klima and Steve Winkelman from the Center for Clean Air Policy published a review of studies into the perceptions that Americans hold about climate change.[2] The authors reviewed multiple studies, and found that:

> [A]pproximately two thirds of Americans think that climate change is occurring ... according to recent surveys from Gallup (52%), Pew (63%), Brookings (65%), Yale (66%), and Stanford (73%).

With percentages ranging from 52% to 73%, James Painter's statement, that "the issue – and the science – of climate change has become contested, polarised, and politicised – at least in the Anglo-Saxon world" rings true. Feeding this contestation is what Painter described as the U.S.'s "pervasive lobbying culture," and action by anti-reformists who have funded conservative think tanks to question climate science.[3] Another mechanism that feeds contestation and public uncertainty about climate change is the media practice of maintaining a "convention of balance," which defaults to giving equal airtime or visual space to both sides of an argument, which misleads public perception despite a weight of evidence on one side or the other.[4] Finally, and despite the convention of balance, Painter showed in his analysis of U.K. print newspapers that climate skepticism is also present in the media, often aligned with the London-based think tank the Global Warming Policy Foundation.[3] In the U.S., voters develop the majority of their news from broadcast media,[4] which according to Kevin Kalhoefer, who found that leading media networks ABC, CBS, NBC, PBS, and Fox News's Sunday program, aired just 50 combined minutes of climate reporting in 2016.[5] The resulting state of societal understanding about climate change can affect organizations both directly and indirectly.

How is societal understanding of and debate about climate change affecting organizations now?

The public's perception and understanding of climate change is affected significantly by other drivers that also need to be examined, namely, media coverage,[4] and lobby groups.[3] Through media and lobby groups, people's perceptions and understanding translate into new markets, and through votes, into government climate change and economic policy. In the U.K. for instance, analysts fear the impact of Brexit on both the British economy and its approach to climate change. If this occurs, any impact on the economy will affect all organizations operating within it. For instance, as long as the main U.K. parties – the Conservatives, Labour, and the Liberal Democrats – continue to pursue climate change policy, the U.K. appears unlikely to drop all targets. However, because its current green economic policies are connected to the European Union Emissions Trading System (EU ETS), any withdrawal from it will affect both the U.K. and the EU, especially because the U.K. is the second-largest source of greenhouse gases in Europe.[6] This situation has created great uncertainty for U.K. organizations that have already invested in green infrastructure and carbon trading and are now needing to pay close attention to future developments that may affect their strategies and investments, especially since they may not be able to recoup their investments in the EU ETS if the U.K. pulls out of the system. The result is that many U.K. organizations are in a state of limbo; uncertain whether green energy or fossil fuel subsidies and prices will be increased or taken away, and whether their assets will become stranded.

In the U.S. similar uncertainty has unfolded as the Trump administration announced the withdrawal from the Paris Climate Accord, although some regions and localities are continuing with their own initiatives, which gives some certainty. At least 14 states and over 200 cities across the U.S. have joined coalitions like America's Pledge, to match Paris Accord targets,[7, 8, 9] which may help to offset any loss of federal funding for clean tech, which is an industry that currently employs 880,000 people nationwide.[10] While uncertainty remains, it is to some small degree currently (at the time of writing) being mitigated for those organizations operating in any of the states and cities that have made the pledge.

How could societal understanding of and debate about climate change affect organizations in 25 years' time?

The short answer is that it depends on the other drivers mentioned above, and the degree to which they will shift public perception; thus it remains perhaps more uncertain than many other drivers in this appendix.

A study by John Cook and colleagues found that just 0.7% of peer-reviewed papers on the topic of climate change they sampled rejected any consensus on climate change science.[11] Whether this, or other studies, are enough to overcome the bias and convention of balance within the media remains to be seen.

In relation to climate change policy, the direction that lobbying could take is important. Since the days that President Madison advocated for the need for interest groups to have a voice in political discourse, lobbying has grown in influence. The voice of corporations, often exercised through campaign financing, was given a considerable boost in 2010 with the U.S. Supreme Court deciding to reject caps on corporate donations,[12] and the political power of corporations has also grown in Europe.[13] It is now often-said that government policy is not only seen as a potential threat, but also as a tool.[14] In his PhD dissertation, Lee Drutman concluded that

> *As a result, corporate lobbying activity is likely to continue to expand for the foreseeable future, with large corporations playing an increasingly central role in the formulation of national policies*[14]

However, there is also a counter-movement that is calling to "get the money out of politics" that grew in strength before the 2016 U.S. elections and continues to gain traction.

The bottom line is that for organizations to prepare for climate change, they need to be aware of the political and cultural attitudes towards climate change in their areas so they can anticipate what kind of policies will be implemented. If organizations want to see economically beneficial green policies, they might want to start influencing public opinion themselves, just as larger players have done for many years.

Socially responsible investing and activist investors

Overview

Socially responsible investing (or SRI) is "the process of integrating personal values and societal concerns into investment decision-making."[15] SRI has a long history, dating back to biblical times when Jewish law gave direction on how to invest ethically,[15] and in the U.S. back to the 17th century, when Quakers refused to hold stock in early trading companies that sold tobacco or alcohol.[16] In his peer-reviewed article investigating SRI in the U.S., President of the First Affirmative Financial Network, Steve Schueth[15] described three main investing strategies: Screening, shareholder advocacy, and community investing. Schueth described screening as the process of excluding or including companies from an investment portfolio on the basis of particular social or environmental criteria important to that investor. The Quakers screened out companies selling tobacco or alcohol. Shareholder advocacy (aka activist investing, or shareholder activism), is the practice of buying shares in publicly traded companies, and using that shareholding to influence management decisions, usually via shareholder resolutions.[15, 17] Lastly, community investing is the practice of providing capital for community development initiatives, with funds usually provided to "low-income, at-risk communities who have difficulty accessing it through conventional channels" through community development funds financial institutions.[15]

SRI has grown exponentially since its beginnings. In the U.S. alone, SRI grew 380% from 1995 to 2009.[16] In 2016, U.S. SRI totaled $8.72 trillion, a 33% rise from 2014 figures.[16] Similar growth has occurred in Europe, where SRI increased 35% yearly from 2009 to 2012.[16] Globally, investors placed $22.89 trillion in SRI in 2016, of which 53% came from Europe and 38% the U.S.[18] In short, SRI is on the rise and shows no signs of slowing down. As Morgan Stanley concluded after 2016 was full of political upheaval, "even in a time of change, interest in sustainable investing appears unflappable. In fact, it's stronger than ever."[19]

Over the last decade, a strong focus has been on integrating concerns about environmental, social, and governance (ESG) into investment decisions,[20] including issues around climate risk and the cost of capital.[21]

How are socially responsible investing and activist investors affecting organizations now?

In the Introduction, I mentioned Ceres, which is a key player in the activist investing world. Ceres typically focuses its energies on influencing the decision-makers of large carbon-intensive companies and those investing in them. For instance, at the end of 2017, it celebrated that four of the top ten asset managers – BlackRock, Vanguard, Fidelity, and American Funds, which manage $12.8 trillion in assets – voted in favor of a climate proposal for the first time in their histories.[22] In addition, three major oil, gas, and electricity companies agreed to create reports detailing their strategies for keeping the Earth under 2°C of global warming. In so doing, these companies were responding to overwhelming shareholder pressure: 67.3% of shareholders at Occidental Petroleum, 62.1% at ExxonMobil, and 56.8% at electricity company PPL Corporation voted to pass these proposals – in Occidental's case, against the wishes of the board.[23] While not legally binding, these proposals are nevertheless pressuring companies to act on climate change, and indicate that companies are being prompted to act by increasingly concerned shareholders who want sustainability as well as returns on their investments.

Even pension funds – despite their primary duties to deliver financial results for their investors – are increasingly screening companies according to ESG criteria; both screening out companies that violate ESG best practices, and screening in those embodying them. Several pension funds, including Calpers in the U.S. and Pensioenfonds Zorg & Welzijn in the Netherlands, screen for ESG factors. In the U.K. and EU legislation requires pension funds to report the role of ESG in their investing decisions,[16] and after the Paris Climate Accord, Sweden's largest pension fund, AP7, sold its investments in six companies it believed violated the Accord: ExxonMobil, Gazprom, TransCanada Corp, Westar, Entergy and Southern Corp.[24] Organizations that do not incorporate ESG criteria in their organizations are starting to have fewer institutional, and individual, investors.

Beyond being a growing trend set to continue, concerns that SRI portfolios have weaker returns no longer seem to apply.[25] Another impact of SRI is that organizations may get better returns on their investments. In 2015, Morgan Stanley concluded that the MSCI Social outperformed the S&P 500 by about 45 points.[26]

How could socially responsible investing and activist investors affect organizations in 25 years' time?

The 2010 U.S. census counted 75 million millennials: Now the largest generation in the country.[27] The first generation in modern history to be worse off than their parents, millennials are nevertheless primed to inherit the largest intergenerational transfer of wealth in human history: anywhere from $24 to 30 trillion by 2020.[28] They are also going to make up 75% of the U.S. workforce by 2025, and the 31% that currently have a 401(k) will certainly rise.[19]

In a recent survey of 200 millennial investors in the U.S. published by Morgan Stanley,[19] 86% expressed interest in SRI generally, and 82% in focusing on climate change specifically. Josh Levin, co-founder of OpenInvest, explains that "Millennials tend to balk at off-the-shelf products. They 'want to express individual values.'"[28] If the Morgan Stanley survey is at all representative, then an overwhelming majority of millennials value the environment. In fact, other research indicates that 75% of millennials believe that their investments could affect climate change, compared with only 58% of the general population.[28]

In 25 years, millennials could plausibly have inherited a great deal of wealth, and be investing it to both state and support their values, and to affect change. This will leave organizations under increasing pressure from millennial customers and investors. Whether or not a business is traded publicly, its adherence to or neglect of ESG factors could plausibly affect its bottom line. To win the trust of skeptical millennials, organizations need to genuinely embrace environmental, social, and governance values.

Technological

Renewable energy and energy efficient technologies

Overview

Technological innovation and climate change combine most readily around energy supply. The energy supply sector is responsible for approximately 35% of global anthropogenic carbon emissions,[29] and with nearly 80% of global energy being supplied by fossil fuels (oil, natural gas, and coal),[30] and with landmark negotiations like the Paris Climate Accord, renewable energy and energy efficient technologies are key to reducing carbon emissions while fulfilling growing demand for energy.

Renewable energy is energy generated from naturally renewable resources, such as sunlight, wind, water or geothermal heat.[30] Renewable energy utilization is on the rise, accounting for 19.2% of global energy consumption in 2014,[31] and the private sector is driving much of the trend as the wholesale price of solar and wind power is becoming increasingly competitive. Energy efficient technologies include products that use less energy per unit of output than their peers, have been produced using energy efficient processes, or those that even cogenerate energy. These technologies include electric and hybrid vehicles, manufacturing equipment, energy efficient appliances, insulation, and other building materials that enable energy saving.

How are renewable energy and energy efficiency technologies affecting organizations now?

Depending on the business you are in, renewable energy and energy efficient technologies can present opportunities to reduce energy costs and carbon emissions, generate your own energy, meet the rising demand for energy efficient products, reduce exposure to energy security issues, sell energy back to the grid, and increase innovation.

Beginning in 2014, influential businesses from across the globe began to publicly commit to transition their companies away from carbon-intensive energy towards renewable energy. In just under three years, 96 of the world's largest companies such as IKEA, Google, and Apple formed the RE100 group,[32] a business collaborative committed to transitioning to 100% renewable energy. For these organizations, renewable energy goes beyond climate change mitigation goals to simply being good for business. For instance, since 2014, founding RE100 member IKEA has reduced its energy costs significantly, and the head of sustainability in the U.K. and Ireland for IKEA, Joanna Yarrow, reported that "becoming 100% renewable is gearing ourselves up to be a successful business in the future."[33]

Another company pursuing renewables is Infosys, a multinational IT firm employing over 200,000 people globally, headquartered in Bengaluru, India. To combat its carbon footprint and address unreliable power, Infosys is working towards generating 100% of its own electricity using renewables,[34] and has also incorporated efficient building design and energy efficient technologies to help reduce emissions. Between 2008 and 2016, Infosys reduced its per capita energy use by 49%. The Executive Vice President of Infosys, Ramadas Kamath, underscored the efficiencies enabled through renewable energy technologies when he stated to the *Economic Times* that "Innovation will be the key to achieve more with less".[35]

Manufacturing companies are also starting to produce products that are either energy efficient, such as cars and even electric trucks being produced by Tesla and Chanje,[36] or carbon neutral products. In 2017, carpet manufacturer Interface went a step further to launch a carbon-negative carpet tile it called "Proof Positive".[37] Interface's Chief Innovation, Marketing and Design Office, Chad Scales, stated that

> *We created this Proof Positive tile to inspire our customers, our industry, and the world to think more broadly about taking on the climate challenge in a new way – to find innovative solutions that will not only reduce, but ultimately reverse global warming.*

How could renewable energy and energy efficiency technologies affect organizations in 25 years' time?

As emerging economies like China and India continue to grow, global demand for energy is expected to surpass supply sometime in the next 20 years.[38] India's energy consumption has doubled since 2000 and India alone is projected to account for a quarter of the expected 48% increase in global energy demand by 2040.[38] This will make renewable energy and energy efficient technologies that much more valuable on the market.

Elena Giannakopoulou and Seb Henbest of Bloomberg New Energy Finance (BNEF) reported in their *New Energy Outlook 2016* that "[b]y 2040, zero-emission energy sources will make up 60% of installed capacity."[39] Over the next several decades, it is projected that industries will continue to push for innovation in energy, with twice as many investment dollars going towards renewable energy technologies compared to fossil fuels.[40] Some analysts, such as Michael Liebreich of BNEF have predicted that renewable energy "will reap 86 percent of the $10.2 trillion likely to be invested in power generation by 2040," because offshore wind turbines are growing in size, and the cost of solar photovoltaic power is dropping.[41]

With demand for clean energy also increasing among consumers,[42] societal and industrial agendas will likely continue to align, and further renewable energy and energy efficiency technologies will continue to emerge.

Water-efficient technologies

Overview

Water-efficient technologies are those that use less water relative to their traditional counterparts, or do other things, such as harvest rainwater, recycle water, help detect leaks, or automatically shut off water flow. They tend to cluster around two main types: "Smart water" devices that rely on cutting-edge computing and electronics to conserve water, and "nature-based solutions"[43] (NBS) that reintroduce pre-industrial methods of drawing from and conserving freshwater sources.

When people think about water scarcity, they often think only about access to clean drinking water; however, domestic water use accounts for only 10% of the amount of water used globally in a given year.[43] Industry consumes the remaining 90% of accessible fresh water; therefore, organizations are on the front lines of both the problem of water scarcity and innovation to mitigate it. According to the UN's World Water Development Report, agriculture accounts for 70% of global water use, making it the sector most affected by – and affecting – water scarcity.[43]

How are water efficiency technologies affecting organizations now?

While every business uses water in some form, agriculture is the sector most responsible for – and therefore most vulnerable to – water scarcity. Unsurprisingly, many water-efficient technologies target irrigation methods and large-scale land use, such as the advanced sprinkler systems identified as "water-efficient technology opportunities" by the U.S. Department of Energy.[44] Automatic shut-off devices use smart water sensors to detect and shut down sprinklers when leaks occur, while multi-rotational sprinklers irrigate fields more evenly, use less water, and produce less runoff. In two 2009 studies, multi-rotational sprinklers were found to reduce water use from 2 inches to less than 1 inch per hour, whereas automatic shut-off devices reduced water use by 39% over 12 months.[45] With water rights and water being a valuable commodity, these technologies enable organizations to save money and water.

Nature-based solutions (NBS) can often be even simpler and cheaper. Farmers in developing countries like Vietnam and Bangladesh have successfully reduced their water use when growing rice simply by monitoring the depth of the rice paddy with a simple plastic pipe and a ruler.[46] By 2011, over 70,000 Filipino farmers and 20,000 from Vietnam and Bangladesh had implemented this simple method, and reduced irrigated water use by between 7 and 25%.[46]

Other industries have prioritized installing water-saving technologies and set significant water-saving goals. To work towards its goal of reducing its global water use by 30% by 2015, Ford Motor Company transformed its engine-building process by working with universities to develop a "drier" way of lubricating cutting tools.[47] Ford also used reverse osmosis technology to recycle wastewater, and hired environmental companies to clean their most polluted water. The result was a 40% reduction in water use at its Hermosillo, Mexico plant from 2000 to 2010 – while production doubled.[47]

Recycling wastewater is also a priority of the world's largest pulp facility, owned and operated by Asia Pulp and Paper (APP) in Jinhai, China.[48] APP developed two patents for demineralizing wastewater – the intellectual property being a potential source of income in addition to the water and money saving technology.[48] As a result, the overall water consumption at the plant has fallen from $32m^3$ per ton of pulp in 2005 to $24m^3$.[48]

How could water efficiency technologies affect organizations in 25 years' time?

Projections of future use of irrigated water varies wildly, from increases of 5.5% up to 42% in 2050 to even a slight decrease due to expectations about water-saving technologies,[49, 50, 51] but the OECD estimates that global water demand for manufacturing could rise as much as 400% by 2050 as developing countries continue to expand their industrial and energy infrastructure.[51]

Water-saving technologies, therefore, could become more important, and as innovations more profitable. They are already a fast-growing market. In 2017, the Global Opportunity Network named smart water technologies as its top sustainability opportunity of the year.[52] Authors of the report proposed that the global market for smart water technology could grow 18.9% annually from US$8.46 billion in 2016 to \$20.10 billion in 2021.[52] Replacing aging infrastructure with more efficient technology could result in \$7–12 billion in savings, as well as saving millions of gallons of water.[52] Organizations that will benefit most would appear to be those developing the patents and manufacturing the hardware, as well as other organizations designing the software; though their customers would also benefit, since more efficient use of water results in reduced water costs.

Nature-based solutions could also continue to grow, as can be seen through recent investments like the creation of the Upper Tana-Nairobi Water Fund in 2015. This public–private partnership was designed to invest in green infrastructure that leans heavily on NBS, such as terracing and reforestation; a business case study predicted that a US\$10 million investment over 10 years would create \$21.5 million of returns for investors.[53] In such scenarios, fund managers would also profit from increasing investment in water-saving technologies, as will forestry, landscaping, and other companies that emphasize green infrastructure that relies on reshaping the land.

Perhaps an overlooked but significant challenge is that of water rights; for example, Native American water rights in the western U.S. comprise over 46 million acre-feet in the heart of the most irrigated section of the country.[54] Such rights may need to be renegotiated in order to maximize the effectiveness of water-saving technologies, since most freshwater sources stretch over thousands of miles.

To conclude, reducing water use would become more and more important if demand outstrips supply, which is often the case in drought-prone areas. Any organizations that use a lot of water could find it harder to function as water becomes more scarce, and incorporating water-saving technologies and NBS could become important.

Economic

Climate-related competition

Overview

In 2017, Business for Social Responsibility noted in its 9th annual survey on the State of Sustainable Business that climate change "is now the top priority, along with human rights, for the first time since 2010."[55] One reason for this is that organizations are starting to compete for customers and employees on the basis of their climate change and sustainability credentials.

How is climate-related competition affecting organizations now?

Climate-related competition is currently affecting organizations in two main ways. First, to build a loyal customer base, businesses are discovering the importance of both delivering energy-efficient products and committing to a wide range of environmentally-responsible practices. Research by The Climate Group "confirms an increasingly receptive market interested in what companies are doing to tackle climate change ... In the U.S. and U.K. ... consumer commitment is rising significantly."[56] The same study found that two-thirds of customers surveyed in the U.S. and U.K. – and over half in China – admire companies that address climate change, and were 5% more likely to purchase a product if told the company was tackling climate change.[56] It also found that "brands that are identified as [climate] leaders inspire ... interest, acceptance, and admiration" as well as "loyalty and trust."[56] A concurrent report from the World Intellectual Property Organization (WIPO) found that almost 70% of around 2,000 people surveyed "would pay a premium for green energy alternatives."[57]

Aside from competing for customers, companies are also finding it increasingly important to commit to reducing their carbon emissions to attract the best talent. Tensie Whelan and Carly Fink argued, based on a study by Magali Delmas and Sanja Pekovic[58] that "21st century employees are focusing more on mission, purpose, and work-life balance," and sustainable practices help create this sense of mission and purpose. Competition for talent helps explain why fossil fuel companies like ExxonMobil and BP stress their efforts to develop renewable energy.[59]

It doesn't hurt, of course, that businesses are saving money by becoming more energy efficient and thus having more capital to spend on advertising campaigns and other key strategic factors. Nick Grant, director of corporate markets and energy services at British Gas, maintains that 20–30% of a business's energy costs – which can be up to 20% of its total expenditures – may be eliminated if energy efficiency is prioritized.[60] Between 2006 and 2010, the top 100 sustainable companies experienced higher sales growth, pre-tax profits, and cash flows in certain sectors compared to other companies, and the revenues of sustainable companies in the S&P Global 100 grew six times more than control companies.[61] Jonah Sachs, the CEO of branding agency Free Range Studios called climate change "a near-guaranteed success for whoever picks up and runs with it."[62]

How could climate-related competition affect organizations in 25 years' time?

As older generations disappear and younger ones grow up, it appears plausible that the current generation gap in beliefs about climate change will also disappear, and beliefs will turn in favor of more climate-change-related competition. In a 2006 article for the journal *Climate Change*, researchers Joni Hersch and W. Kip Viscusi examined this gap in a survey of over 14,000 residents of 15 European nations.[63] The researchers discovered that respondents aged 15–24 were twice as willing to pay higher fuel costs than those aged 65 and over. Such generational gaps in understanding of and concern about climate change are also notable in the United States, as Dana Nuccitelli highlighted in a report in the *Bulletin of Atomic Scientists*.[64] 63% of survey participants expressed a willingness to pay more – up to $20 per month – to see governmental greenhouse gas regulations, but the numbers change markedly when broken down for political affiliation and age: 78% of Democrats 40 or younger favored the proposal, compared to just 62% for those over 65; similarly, 61% of Republicans under 50 supported the policy, as opposed to just 44% for those over 50.[64] In Australia, the climate change gap is even more startling: 70% of 18–24 year-olds believed climate change was real in a 2014 ABC news poll, as opposed to 39% of 65 year-olds and over.[65] These attitudes of younger people will affect what they buy as consumers in the future, and for whom they are willing to work.

In relation to work, in their *Harvard Business Review* article on creating a top workplace, Rob Goffee and Gareth Jones wrote that "people want to be a part of something bigger than themselves, something they can believe in."[66] When coupled with the generational gap noted above, this suggests that younger generations will continue to see benefits in mitigating climate change,[66] and as they grow older begin to enact their beliefs through their career decisions. Organizations that can attract talented employees through climate-related competition, and if the organization can live up to the employees' ideals, the employees will also be happier, which will in turn benefit the organization. For instance, Whelan and Fink noted that organizations with transparent and comprehensive sustainability policies can experience higher employee morale and loyalty, and lower turnover than other companies; resulting in savings of up to 90–200% of an employee's annual salary for each retained worker.[61]

In conclusion, climate change competition could become more important to organizations in future, not only in relation to competing for business, but also competing for talent.

Public–private partnerships

Overview

Public–private partnerships (PPP) are long-term contracts between a public agency – a local, regional, or national government or government-owned entity – and private companies.[67] PPPs are most often used for long-term, expensive infrastructure projects, such as transportation and energy infrastructure.[68] This makes PPPs an ideal vehicle for many climate projects, and as Vipul Bhagat and Ari Skromme of the World Bank's International Finance Corporation noted:

> *Many of today's climate-related infrastructure projects are PPPs by definition, even if the partnership is not explicit. In fact, addressing climate issues from a business perspective is by default a PPP, because there is almost always some kind of a regulatory connection.*[69]

With PPPs, both sectors share the risk and rewards; the public agency avoids lengthy delays due to intermittent funds and maintains regulatory control and ownership, while the private sector reaps the profits and can test and implement innovative methods that will bring it more customers.[68]

How are PPPs affecting organizations now?

Organizations have much to gain by entering into climate-related PPPs, since the projects tend to be long term and expensive, offering organizations lengthy, lucrative contracts, and organizations are encouraged to be innovative in these agreements. One of the reasons PPPs work for both sectors is that public agencies have less money and incentive to invest in new approaches to combating climate change, while organizations like construction companies, private utilities, and civil engineering and architecture firms get opportunities to innovate.

One PPP example is the 20-year Power Purchasing Agreement (PPA) that Washington, D.C. signed with Iberdrola Renewables in 2015 to supply the district with wind power.[70] At the time, this deal was the largest of its kind by an American city, enabling Washington, D.C. to access wind power without having to build a wind farm. The 125–150,000MWh of wind power purchased annually would cost 30% less than traditional fossil fuels, and reduce greenhouse gas emissions by at least 17% from 2013 levels.[71] Washington, D.C. becomes a greener city, while Iberdrola Renewables has a long-term customer for its wind power that will enable it to pursue further innovations in delivering clean energy.

Despite Washington, D.C.'s ground-breaking PPA, the U.S. has been less inclined to adopt PPPs than other regions of the world. Between 1985 and 2011, there were 377 PPP infrastructure projects valued at US$68.4 billion nationwide; in contrast, European countries spent $353.3 billion on PPPs over the same quarter-century.[67] Nevertheless, PPPs will likely grow in popularity even in the U.S. as their applicability to climate-related issues and infrastructural projects become increasingly clear. As the Washington, D.C. wind PPA indicates, cities are finding PPPs an attractive way to implement climate adaptation plans. New York has also launched a 10-year infrastructure renovation plan to "transform New York City's buildings for a low-carbon future."[72] The plan's multiple initiatives aim to reduce GHG levels by 30% by 2025 and 80% by 2050.[72]

As an example of the kind of economic impact such plans can have, New York City estimates that an Energy-Performance Contract partnership between the City's Housing Authority, the U.S. Department of Housing and Urban Development, and local utilities to make buildings more energy efficient should create 18,000 new jobs and $1.9 billion in yearly economic activity by 2030.[72] Any business that becomes a part of the plan will likely end up with a lucrative, long-term contract that will participate in a project to make New York City greener and built to last in a more challenging climate future.

To see the benefits from an organization's perspective, we can look at the Hindustan Construction Company (HCD) in India. Founded nearly 100 years ago, HCC has built a majority of India's major infrastructure projects, including 65% of its nuclear plants, 28% of its hydroelectric power plants, 365 bridges, and over 3600km of highways and 300km of tunnels.[73] In 2007, it was the first Indian company to sign the "CEO Water Mandate," a public–private initiative launched by the United Nations Global Compact (UNGC) at the World Economic

Forum.[73] By adopting the 4-R water principle of reduce, recycle, reuse, and recharge, HCC has revolutionized the way it uses water for its major infrastructure projects – saving money and garnering extensive global praise and attention in the process. In one project to build an expressway from Delhi to Faridabad, HCC harvested rainwater in an historically dry region using traditional means, like roof-top catchments and ponds, and designed a means of recharging local aquifers with runoff from the expressway itself.[74] Secure in its contract to maintain the express-way for 18 years, HCC felt able to experiment with such innovative ideas, and the success will likely help it win more contracts in the future – especially since the company predicts that the expressway will eventually conserve more water than was consumed during its construction.[75]

On the potential downsides of PPPs, in its Caring for Climate report,[75] the UN Global Compact and Environment Programme reported challenges, such as lack of cost-benefit information, to implementing successful climate change adaptation policies.[75] In India a cautionary tale exists in the presence of Coca-Cola in Kala-dera, in the desert state of Rajasthan. The 2012 Caring for Climate report cele-brated the company's work at its 56 bottling plants in India, directly employing 25,000 people.[75] Moreover, Coca-Cola had prioritized water scarcity as early as 2004 and made Water Source Vulnerability Assessments a requirement of all plants in 2008.[75] However, Coca-Cola shut the Kaladera plant in February 2016 after lengthy battles with local, community-led campaigns accusing the company of depleting the region's precious groundwater resources since 2003.[76] These kinds of troubles indicate that PPPs can go sour if companies put profits ahead of the common good.

How could PPPs affect organizations in 25 years' time?

Exactly how PPPs will impact organizations in the future will depend on how public sector policies and approaches to climate change adapt in the face of wor-sening weather and rising public pressure. Adaptation projects may become the PPP norm if climate change mitigation efforts are seen as less effective over time, which would create major infrastructure projects across the globe. We can cur-rently see a push towards private sector renewable energy projects in low- to middle-income countries like India.[77]

Edouard Perard, Regional Coordinator for South Asia at the World Bank's Public-Private Infrastructure Advisory Facility noted that PPPs focusing on adap-tation-related infrastructure renovation and construction are rising in popularity because they can immediately improve people's lives and the environment.[77] Since these kinds of projects often last 25 years or more, they can address medium- and long-term issues while offering private companies an opportunity to lock in long-term work and profits.[77] In future, both developed and developing nations could use PPPs more often.

As Dean Koh makes clear in his article on PPPs:

the implications are that governments can no longer be passive or reactive in a technologically-driven economy. It is imperative that governments embrace change and disruption through deliberate collaboration and partnerships with private sectors, in order to stay relevant and continue to facilitate processes that would make a positive impact on the economy and keep their citizens engaged.[68]

Ecological

Sea level change

Overview

Sea level change refers to global and local changes in sea levels, and is defined by the IPCC as follows:

> *Sea level can change, both globally and locally due to (i) changes in the shape of the ocean basins, (ii) a change in ocean volume as a result of a change in the mass of water in the ocean, and (iii) changes in ocean volume as a result of changes in ocean-water density.*[78]

Sea level change poses significant risks for organizations with operations, assets, suppliers, or markets, or relying on transport and utility infrastructure in coastal regions or low-lying inland areas. NASA's analysis of changing sea levels indicates that sea levels have risen 7cm (2.75in) globally over the past 22 years.[79] Rising sea levels cause higher tides, and exacerbate storm surge during extreme weather events.

How is sea level change affecting organizations now?

Impacts of sea level rise include increased exposure to flooding and flood-related property damage, thus, increasing repair, maintenance, and insurance costs, as well as reduced revenue if business is disrupted. Insurance companies are already experiencing insurances losses connected to sea level change. Assets may also depreciate or appreciate in value, depending on whether they are on low or high ground, respectively.

The World Resources Institute noted that South-East Florida has experienced 12in (30.5cm) of sea level rise since 1870.[80] The effects of sea level change are already affecting Miami, where saltwater regularly floods city streets at high tide, and threatens the drinking water supply.[81] The Union of Concerned Scientists' interactive online map of sea level rise[82] shows that much of Miami's coastline already floods around 26 times per year. While all organizations are affected, the owners of and building management companies servicing Florida's luxury condo and hotel buildings are on the front lines. Katherine Kallergis reported in *South Florida Real Estate News* that some of Miami Beach's buildings, such as the "Crimson, Carillon and Ritz-Carlton Bal Harbour" are just 2ft (60cm) above sea level, and have been identified as vulnerable to flooding.[83] The BBC reported that

Miami's coastal properties already experience regular tidal flooding (including country clubs north of Miami).[84] The Union of Concerned Scientists reported that Florida Citizens (the state's largest insurer), which insures 62% of Florida's commercial and residential multi-unit dwelling market, has seen its loss exposure grow "from about $155 Billion to almost $500 Billion over the last 10 years." Correspondingly, neighborhoods on higher ground are increasing in value and are gentrifying, as people seek to leave their low-lying property and look for homes on higher ground.[85]

News from Egypt also suggests that a similar phenomenon is occurring in the Nile River Delta. Jane Arraff reported for NPR[86] that retailers, tourism operators, farmers, and governments in the Nile River Delta have all been affected by loss of business and crops due to flooding and salination, river bank erosion, saltwater erosion of delicate historic buildings, and the need to construct sea wall barriers.

Many organizations are incorporating sea level change into their planning, particularly since the U.S. Securities and Exchange Commission provided guidelines for climate risk disclosure. For example, before it was identified as the first climate-change-induced bankruptcy in January 2019 (due to wildfires), California utility company PG&E Corporation reported its long-term risk of "higher flooding and inundation potential at coastal and low elevation facilities due to sea level rise combined with high tides, storm runoff and storm surges."[87]

How could sea level change affect organizations in 25 years' time?

Future sea level change will be driven in part by land-based ice sheets and glaciers in Greenland and Antarctica melting into oceans, and by the warming and expanding of existing ocean water.[88] A team of scientists led by James Hansen at the Columbia University Earth Institute[89] recently found that water flowing into oceans from melting ice sheets and glaciers also exacerbates ice sheet erosion by causing more precipitation.

Global sea levels are predicted to continue rising "well beyond 2100."[90] They are estimated to rise by 3ft (91cm) on average over the next 100–200 years, which indicates that sea level change of 9in (23cm) is plausible over the next 25 to 50 years.[88] The Union for Concerned Scientists' interactive map[82] suggests that in 2035, under moderate sea level rise, more of Miami's shoreline will be flooded regularly, and in 2060 the majority of Miami Beach will be affected. In Miami real estate news outlet *The Real Deal*, Erik Bojnansky reported that real estate professionals are already anticipating Miami Beach property values to fall,[91] with some estimating that Miami property stands to lose up to US$3.5 Trillion in value.[92]

Like many climate change issues, there may be winners and losers. For instance, building and maintaining pumps, sea walls, dikes, levees, and other infrastructure aiming to protect existing assets and infrastructure in vulnerable areas will require billions of dollars per year. By 2100, the cost to the U.S. is estimated to reach at least US$12 billion and possibly US$71 billion if preventative measures are not taken now.[93] Either way, engineering companies, construction companies, environmental consultants, town planners, and others will likely find themselves with plenty of work. Organizations servicing gentrifying areas on high ground will experience changes to market demographics, needs, and expectations, while those that service flood-prone areas may see their customers relocating elsewhere and operational problems due to key infrastructure being affected. Insurance companies and development project financiers will plausibly rethink their ability to insure and finance coastal developments. Owners of vulnerable assets, such as Miami's Ritz-Carlton Bal Harbour noted above will benefit from actively seeking out partnerships with cities and counties to understand their vulnerabilities and decide the best course of action.

Rising temperature

Overview

The IPCC refers to temperature as "[t]he globally averaged combined land and ocean surface temperature,"[30] and estimates that people and industry "have caused approximately 1.0°C of global warming above pre-industrial levels."[90] Global averaged temperature rose by an average of 0.85°C between 1880 and 2012.[30] Rising temperature produces more frequent hot extremes and fewer cold extremes, and influences many other climate change drivers, including: Warming oceans increasing the intensity of extreme storms and reducing the amount of sea ice, warming waters expanding and exacerbating sea level rise, warming atmosphere producing more rain and less snow, evaporation over land increasing the severity of drought, wildfires, and surface water salination, and changes in the distribution of pests and diseases, which affects crops, trees, and human health.

How are rising temperatures affecting organizations now?

Temperature rise has doubled the probability of heat waves in some regions,[30] and reduced worker safety and productivity during heat waves may be one of the most immediate effects of temperature rise,[94] which can affect the bottom line through project delays and increased insurance costs. Outdoor-oriented industries, such as construction, are particularly vulnerable, but others may also be affected where the demand for air conditioning causes blackouts or curtailment. Blackouts are already affecting industrial power users. For example, an Australian paper mill, an aluminum smelter, and local water treatment operators were forced to temporarily halt operations in February 2017, when temperatures climbed to 117°F (47°C) in parts of the country.[95]

Adding to this, increasing temperature is already affecting farmers, food producers, and other organizations. For instance, temperature increase exacerbated droughts in India between 2000 and 2002. Crops failed and over a million people were left hungry or were otherwise affected in the region of Orissa.[96] In British Columbia, the same warming winters that helped farmers in the Okanagan Valley shift into wine production, as discussed in the Introduction, have produced significant effects in the timber industry. Researchers at the University of Northern British Columbia[97] have examined how warming winters enabled the Mountain Pine Beetle to flourish, infest, and kill much of the forest area in the British Columbia interior. The infestation led to increased felling by timber companies in an attempt to salvage the wood.

How could rising temperatures affect organizations in 25 years' time?

Surface temperature is predicted to rise 2.5–7.8°C by 2100 regardless of global mitigation measures, and is estimated to increase further if global mitigation measures are not implemented.[30] This could mean a roughly 0.75–2.0°C change in the next 25 years, which would stress land and ocean-based food sources. Farms in high-latitude locations will benefit from temperature increases by the mid-21st century, while production of staples such as wheat, rice, and maize may suffer in tropical and temperate regions,[30] which could affect food production companies, aid organizations, and others relying on them. A paper recently published in *Economics of Disasters and Climate Change* by an international research team projected that "climate change could reduce global crop production by 9% in the 2030s and by 23% in the 2050s,"[98] which suggests significant plausible change in the availability of staple ingredients.

Fishing businesses and fishing communities relying on ocean fish stock may also be positively or adversely affected by temperature rise. By the mid-21st century, as oceans warm, significant marine life migration may be evident as species move to pursue their preferred temperature range and new species move in. The IPCC projects that fish stocks may grow at mid to high latitudes and decline at tropical latitudes, and that ocean fish production will shift globally by 2100,[30] indicating that impacts may be noticeable in 25 years.

Adding to this, coastal tourism may suffer as thermal stress is one climate-related issue facing coral reefs.[99] UNESCO predicts that without global climate mitigation, coral reefs could be extinct by 2100,[100] which would have grave effects on a wide range of coastal tourist destinations before that time, including in 25 years' time. Scientists in the Florida Keys are already working to try to save the local coral reef, which is key to Florida's tourism industry.[101]

The IPCC[30] has stated there is a moderate risk of temperature-related events also occurring at lower temperature increases of 1–2°C above pre-industrial levels, and the Paris Climate Accord aims to limit global warming to 2°C above pre-industrial temperatures for this reason.

Changes in precipitation (including drought)

Overview

Precipitation refers to "rain, drizzle, dew, hail, snow and other forms of moisture from the atmosphere which reaches the ground."[102] Changes in precipitation over time can affect organizations directly and indirectly, and are related to other potential drivers including drought, wildfires, extreme weather, temperature change, and water policy. For instance, the IPCC is reasonably certain that in some areas evaporation has made saline surface water more saline since the 1950s, and that increased precipitation in other areas has made low-saline water fresher.[30] Further, the frequency and intensity of heavy precipitation events has likely increased worldwide over the last 60 years,[30] and in the U.S., heavy precipitation events have increased by 74% in the Northeast and 26% in the Southeast.[103]

How are changes in precipitation affecting organizations now?

In the United States, the recent drought in California, which was discussed in the Introduction in relation to Blue Diamond Growers, was due to lack of rain. Texas and Oklahoma were also drought-affected, and in 2011, when temperatures rose above 100°F for 100 days, water depletion caused over $10 billion in direct losses to agriculture businesses.[104] In addition to this, the cost of flood damage has been rising globally since the 1970s, and increased exposure of populations and infrastructure to flood risk accounts for a part of this increase.[30] Floods killed 500,000 people and affected more than 2.8 billion others worldwide between 1980 and 2009, and in the U.S., the average cost of damage to property and crops between 1981 and 2011 was almost $8 billion annually.[104]

According to analysis by ClimateWise, a global network of insurance industry organizations, more frequent storms with heavy precipitation are causing uninsured losses to rise by making some assets uninsurable, or costly to insure. The 2016 ClimateWise[105] report *Investing for Resilience* found that the "protection gap" between the costs of natural disasters and the amount insured had quadrupled since the 1980s. While the effects of insurance gaps mostly affect property and casualty insurers, the National Association of Insurance Commissioners' *Climate Risk Disclosure Survey*[106] reported that life and health insurance companies are also beginning to examine their climate exposure and disclose their climate risk management practices.

How could changes in precipitation affect organizations in 25 years' time?

The nature of precipitation may continue to change, particularly if more of it falls in extreme events. The IPCC currently assesses the risk of extreme precipitation events and coastal flooding as moderate, and this will increase if the predicted 1°C of additional average temperature increase occurs.[30] Overall, you will need to investigate research in your local region, because changes in precipitation will be uneven. High latitudes, the equatorial Pacific, and mid-latitude wet regions are expected to receive more precipitation by 2100, which will equate to moderate increases in the next 25 years; however, mid-latitude and subtropical dry regions may experience decreased mean precipitation, while monsoons and other extreme precipitation events are expected to expand their geographic reach and produce more rain.[30]

At the other end of the spectrum, some areas will receive significantly less precipitation than in previous years. In the U.S. South-West, precipitation could drop by as much as 15% by 2080,[30] which will reduce the amount of water available for drinking, agriculture, industrial use, and power generation.[30, 107] From a food production perspective, grapes, lettuce, pecans, and wheat are all valuable crops grown in this area,[108] and these and others would all require additional irrigation, and perhaps the purchase of additional water rights by producers, to remain viable.

In some areas, shifting precipitation patterns will also likely decrease tree density,[30] which would affect the lumber and wood products industries by reducing the viability of these areas for wood production, which could have cascading effects for the availability and cost of building materials in affected areas. Other organizations, such as national parks and nature reserves, also stand to be affected by this issue.

Extreme weather

Overview

In its 2014 report on impacts, adaptation, and vulnerability, the IPCC[94] defined extreme weather as follows:

> An extreme weather event is an event that is rare at a particular place and time of year … By definition, the characteristics of what is called extreme weather may vary from place to place … When a pattern of extreme weather persists for some time, such as a season, it may be classed as an extreme climate event, especially if it yields an average or total that is itself extreme (e.g., drought or heavy rainfall over a season).

While drought can also be extreme weather, it was covered in another summary, so here I will cover other extreme weather events, in particular storms. It is worth noting that these events are related to other drivers – namely sea level change and rising ocean temperatures.[109]

Hurricane activity has increased in the North Atlantic since 1970.[94] Researchers have historically attributed this trend to increasing wealth and burgeoning populations in affected areas. However, in a 2015 paper published in *Nature Geoscience*, Francisco Estrada and his colleagues from Universidad Nacional Autónoma, Mexico, and VU University in the Netherlands found that "[i]n 2005, US$2 to US$14 billion of the recorded annual losses could be attributable to climate change, 2 to 12% of that year's normalized losses".[110] IPCC data also shows increases in frequency, intensity, and duration of hurricanes, particularly since the early 1980s, even taking into account improvements in satellite-based remote sensing techniques.[94]

How is extreme weather affecting organizations now?

The economic losses caused by U.S. hurricanes have risen since 1900.[110] A single storm has the power to inflict enormous damage and wreak havoc on industry. For instance, Hurricane Katrina was one of the deadliest and most costly hurricanes on record,[111] affecting over 93,000sqm,[112] killing over 1,800 people, and displacing 1.3 million.[113] Originally a Category 1 hurricane when it hit Florida, Hurricane Katrina returned to Gulf waters and became a Category 5, then weakened to Category 3 before making its second landfall.[111] Unlike most other hurricanes, however, Katrina did not weaken soon after it hit land.[112] In addition to the storm surge, damaging winds, and rainfall, Katrina generated 43 reported tornadoes.[111] Katrina dealt $160 billion in damage (adjusted to 2017 dollars),[114] and left roughly three million people and businesses without electricity, in some cases for weeks.[111] There was extensive damage to facilities and infrastructure, as well as power interruptions. These conditions temporarily devastated the oil and gas, tourism, hospitality, and fishing industries by displacing suppliers, the companies themselves, as well as markets. For instance, Christine Rushton reported in *USA Today* that the high degree of population displacement created a labor shortage that affected businesses on the Gulf Coast.[113]

More recently, Hurricane Harvey, which hit Houston and south-east Texas in August 2017, has become the second-most costly hurricane, causing $125 billion in damage (in 2017 dollars),[114] with similar devastating physical damage. Like Katrina, Hurricane Harvey affected many organizations. Insurance companies were hit with the wave of damage claims, and a secondary wave of dissatisfied businesses battling with them to recover lost income.[115] Others called for the Federal Flood Risk Management Standard to be reinstated.[116] Small business author and columnist, Rhonda Abrams, estimates that small businesses affected by Harvey and other storms face higher insurance rates, loss of business, resource shortages, and higher taxes.[117]

How could extreme weather affect organizations in 25 years' time?

Climate models project an increase in the number of the strongest (Category 4 and 5) hurricanes.[109] At current levels of adaptation and risk reduction, the IPCC estimates that the risk of damage to buildings and displacement in urban areas is medium in the near term (2030–2040), and high to very high in the longer term (2080–2100).[30]

These impacts could cause insurance payouts to rise, and subsequently insurance premiums to rise and organizations could become more vulnerable if they have assets in areas that are exposed to coastal or inland flooding, storm surge, wind, rain, as well as interrupted energy, internet, infrastructure, and transport services associated with extreme weather. Organizations could also experience more severe supply chain and market disruptions.

Political/legal

International climate change policy

Overview

In 1992, the United Nations Framework Convention on Climate Change (UNFCCC) was formed to negotiate an international treaty to curb anthropogenic carbon emissions to prevent dangerous climate change.[118] The overarching goal is to keep global warming to less than 2°C (ideally, 1.5°C).[119] Article 3.1 of the UNFCCC states that developed countries "should take the lead in combating climate change," while Article 3.3 states that "where there are threats of serious or irreversible damage, lack of full scientific certainty should not be used as an excuse for postponing action."[118]

In 2005, the Kyoto Protocol was ratified, and bound developed countries to reduce their emissions to 5.2% below 1990 levels by 2012.[118] The Kyoto Protocol is facilitated by three mechanisms that provide parties to the agreement various ways to reduce their emissions: Emissions trading; Joint implementation; and the Clean Development Mechanism.[118]

One challenge of the Kyoto Protocol is that it was negotiated in stages and relied on multiple commitment periods – 2008–2012, then 2013–2020 – which have not provided enough incentive for some governments to invest in long-term upgrades to energy, transport, water, and other infrastructure to reduce their carbon emissions.[120] The 2015 Paris Agreement aimed to strengthen the global response by requiring all parties to declare their emission reduction efforts through "nationally determined contributions" to 2030, to report regularly on their emissions, and strengthen their implementation efforts.[118]

International agreements filter down to organizations via policy created at national, regional, and local governments. For instance, in 2008, India developed a National Action Plan on Climate Change that includes mitigation and adaptation initiatives,[121] including a goal to increase solar energy to 100 gigawatts by 2022.[122] As a result, there has been a marked increase in both large-scale and rooftop solar, and the rooftop market alone is presently worth $US30 billion.[123] India also has a vibrant energy market, as demand for energy continues to grow by 6–7% per annum, and renewable energy is estimated to grow by 25% annually, which represents an enormous market for suppliers.[124] By comparison, the U.S. has waivered in its commitment to the international treaty, which has introduced uncertainty for organizations needing to make long-term investment decisions. The U.S. plays an important role in the global response to climate change because both its economy and carbon footprint are large;[125] however, it has not ratified the Kyoto Protocol, and the Trump administration opted out of the Paris Agreement.[126] Adding to the uncertainty is that even though the U.S. left the Paris Agreement, it still has obligations until 2020[126] that include reporting its NDCs.[125] In response to uncertainty generated at the national level, 35+ U.S. states have created their own renewable energy targets, and 25+ have set their own energy efficiency targets.[127]

As climate change is estimated to intensify over the second half of the 21st century,[90] governments and businesses will need to adopt low-carbon policies and practices to mitigate the effects of global warming on humanity. A 2007 meta-analysis estimated that the cost of lowering CO_2 emissions to keep global warming under 2°C – the threshold beyond which the effects of global warming are projected to become catastrophic – varied on average from a 3.4% loss of global GDP to an *increase* of 3.9%.[128] As a decade has passed without significant international action on climate change, however, these statistics are likely optimistic. As the international community continues to delay on climate change policy these costs may rise.

How is international climate change policy affecting organizations now?

In the absence of a binding global policy on climate change to which nations will adhere, the effects on organizations depend on a number of variables, including the type of business and policies in place (or being developed) where it is located. Perhaps surprisingly, organizations in areas with comprehensive climate change policies already in place often do as well – or even better – compared to their counterparts in areas without them. The carbon tax implemented in British Columbia, Canada's westernmost province, in 2008 is an example of how climate change policies can go hand-in-hand with economic success. During the first six years of this revenue-neutral tax, BC saw fuel consumption drop 16% while also having the lowest personal income tax rate in Canada and one of the lowest corporate tax rates in the OECD.[129] BC's GDP growth over this period was higher than the rest of Canada: growing a total of 1.75% over 2008–2013, compared to 1.28% for the country.[130] In contrast, societies that have been lax about implementing climate change policies have experienced economic losses. The Global Commission on the Economy and Climate, for instance, estimates that the top 15 CO_2-emitting nations lost an average of 4.4% of GDP in 2010 due to mortalities caused by air pollution.[131] Furthermore, claims of adverse effects by industries like agriculture have not been supported by the research.[132] A 2009 study by McKinsey & Company concluded that businesses save money in the long-term the sooner they replace current technology with low-carbon alternatives.[133] Organizations are incurring fewer losses and seeing economic gains when they are proactive in adopting low-carbon policies, indicating that investing now can help save money in the long term.

It has been argued by energy-intensive companies, and my own research suggests it will continue to be argued, that energy policies supporting a low-carbon future will significantly depreciate the value of assets, and adversely affect profits.[134] Indeed, if you are in a carbon-intensive industry there are potential threats on both these fronts that you should examine. However, climate policies are presenting significant opportunities to those producing renewable energy technologies, and also to others in the value chain, such as organizations supplying biomass to bioenergy power plants.[135] The global market for renewable and low carbon technologies is reported now to be worth \$US5.5 trillion,[136] and in the U.S. wavering national policy has not dampened state and local policy commitments that have increased opportunities in solar,[137] biodiesel,[138] and ethanol.[139]

Climate policies often manifest within organizations as energy initiatives such as committing to sourcing 100% renewable energy, or investing in energy efficient buildings, transport, appliances, and machinery, or developing energy efficient products. For instance, companies are working to create demand for more than 100 terawatt-hours of renewable electricity.[140] One such company is General Motors, which has a goal to use 100% renewable electricity by 2050, and another is Bank of America, which aims to be carbon neutral and source 100% renewable electricity by 2020. Another – Apple – already uses 93% renewable electricity, and has committed to install more than 4GW of new clean energy worldwide by 2020.

Initiatives such as these create opportunities for suppliers of energy-efficient products. For instance, a 2013 study by Carlos López-Gómez and colleagues[141] suggested that by 2020 six in ten light bulbs will be LEDs, and that conversion of biomass into fuels, energy, and chemicals has the potential to generate over US $230 billion. Further opportunities include new leasing and financing models like "Solar-as-a-Service," where retail customers can lease panels if they cannot afford (or have no subsidies available for) the upfront costs. Residential solar installations have shown steady growth since 2010–2011, and publicly listed companies like SolarCity, Sunrun, and Vivint had collectively deployed 3000 megawatts of energy by the fourth quarter of 2015.[142] The broader sector employed over 200,000 people by 2016.[143]

In relation to transport, research by Goldman Sachs[142] suggests that the incentivization of electric vehicles (EV) and plug-in hybrids could include the deployment of charging infrastructure, and other benefits, such as free parking and the right to use bus lanes, as well as tax exemptions and subsidies. Such a trend could bring potential opportunities for organizations in or surrounding EV and hybrid vehicle production and maintenance. On the other hand, electric vehicles and hybrids present potential threats to those producing and maintaining vehicles relying on fossil fuels, and most of the big carmakers have developed EV and hybrid capabilities over the past two decades.

How could international climate change policy affect organizations in 25 years' time?

The IPCC has estimated that "limiting global warming to 1.5°C … would require rapid and far-reaching transitions in energy, land, urban and infrastructure (including transport and buildings), and industrial systems," and that current emission levels will not meet the goal.[90] The UN Environment Program estimates that developing nations in particular could spend up to $140–300 billion per year by 2030 and $280–500 billion per year by 2050 on adaptation measures, and organizations of all kinds would be needed to implement these changes.[144] Since up to 75% of the global population will likely live in cities by 2050, demand for city planners, engineers, and construction firms who specialize in sustainable infrastructure could increase in both developing and developed nations.[145] Similarly, companies involved in reforestation and soil regeneration could be needed in large numbers to enhance natural carbon sinks.[128] Agricultural companies that develop, grow, and harvest crops resistant to extreme weather conditions would also be needed. In addition, law and public policy firms that specialize in environmental issues would be in more demand as low-carbon policy becomes the dominant political and economic issue worldwide.

Conversely, it is plausible that organizations that rely on carbon-intensive technologies would need to overhaul their infrastructure to become low-carbon. Fossil fuel companies could see their fortunes change swiftly the longer they delay developing low-carbon energy sources; the need to curb CO_2 emissions could lead to removal of the $550B in global subsidies the sector receives each year, and even replacement of them with carbon taxes and permits.[146]

To sustain global mitigation efforts, policies incentivizing renewable energy, and carbon sequestration technologies and initiatives such as reforestation could continue to grow, creating opportunities for many types of organizations. For instance, while carbon capture and storage seems unlikely to be commercially viable until 2030,[147] it could create an industry with an annual turnover of US$48–108 billion.[135] Further developments in battery technologies could gear the auto industry towards cleaner vehicles with improved efficiency and reduced emissions.[141] López-Gómez and colleagues[141] indicated in their report that resource scarcity could also further drive the emergence of an "eco-sector" surrounding water management, renewable energy, and recycling and waste management. Its global market is currently estimated at US$1.2 trillion and is expected to reach US$8.44 trillion worldwide over the next 20 years.

In conclusion, while international climate agreements and national climate policies remain less certain, much research points towards better outcomes for those organizations that can navigate how policies in their region may affect them in future.

Water policy

Overview

Consultant on water issues, Josh Newton, described water as "the principal medium through which climate change expresses itself, particularly through intensified floods and droughts."[148] With this backdrop, water policy refers to the government of water resources provision, the use of water, disposal of wastewater, and other decisions to ensure the sustainability of water resources in a given region. Climate change has perhaps no greater impact than through the water cycle, making water management one of the most important professions now and for the foreseeable future.[149]

Water is essential to human life, and therefore to business survival as well. Organizations may depend directly on water as a production input and for their livelihood, such as agriculture, utilities, transportation, water tourism,[149] hotels, and restaurants, or indirectly on account of them employing people who need access to clean drinking water.[150] In the U.S., for instance, water utilities provide freshwater to 86% of the population and nearly half of commercial and industrial organizations.[150] Access to clean drinking water in particular saves money on multiple levels, because without it, a single outbreak of water-borne illness is estimated to cost over US$100 million in medical costs,[151] while the potential productivity losses are also significant.[152] The U.S. Environmental Protection Agency estimated that 71% of productivity losses between 1971 and 2000 were due to drinking water contamination outbreaks.[152]

How is water policy affecting organizations now?

In 2016, the American Society for Civil Engineers (ASCE) reported that the U.S. needs to invest at least $123 billion yearly over the next decade to repair its ailing water infrastructure.[150] Moreover, it estimated that "the average US business loses $230 in sales *per employee*" each day that water service is disrupted – a daily loss of $43.5 billion in sales and $22.5 billion in GDP at the national level. For water-dependent organizations – like recreational boating and fishing companies, which generate $70 billion yearly in sales and employ over 150,000 people, sales can drop by 75% per day, or as much as $5800 per employee.[150] Thus, organizations can lose a lot of revenue anytime their local water supplies are disrupted.

On one hand organizations and residents may celebrate that U.S. federal funding for water infrastructure is low – just 9% of total capital spending in 2014, down from 63% in 1977[150] – because it keeps taxes low. However, knowing that water infrastructure is critical, local governments and taxpayers nonetheless pick up the slack at some point, and local governments had increased spending on water to $100 per person in 2014, up from $45 in 1977.[150]

While there are direct and indirect impacts for all kinds of organizations, water organizations are some of the most affected. On one hand, the current U.S. administration has articulated plans to privatize water utilities, which presents opportunities for water companies. However, on the other hand concerns about prioritizing profits over safety have been raised, which potentially affect their branding and bottom line. For instance, Michelle Chen, writing for *The Nation*, noted how French company Veolia has faced lawsuits and accusations both of overcharging and of failing federal water safety standards in Indianapolis and Gladwater, TX, respectively.[153] Moreover, the writers of the Mayors Innovation Project 2016 noted that private utilities charge 14% more than public utilities.[154]

How could water policy affect organizations in 25 years' time?

How much water policies will affect organizations in future depends upon the kinds of infrastructure changes implemented now. In 2012, the American Water Works Association (AWWA) published a study that estimated a cost of $1 trillion over 25 years to repair the nation's drinking water infrastructure.[155] The study estimated that replacing pipes would cost the most, up to 84% of the $278 billion needed to repair infrastructure in the Northeast and Midwest, while population growth comprised 62% of the $277 billion needed to expand clean drinking water access to the South and West.[156] The study predicted that water bills could rise anywhere from $300 to $550 over 2012 levels to pay for these improvements.[156]

However, there is an upside to the need to repair America's ailing water infrastructure: Job creation. Using the ACSE's 2016 figure of $82 billion over 10 years needed to repair U.S. water systems, the Value of Water Campaign calculated that implementing such a plan would produce more than $220 billion in total economic activity and 1.3 million jobs in that decade.[156] Moreover, investments in an upgraded water system with fewer leaks and greater energy efficiency could save organizations nearly $94 billion yearly in sales over the same amount of time.[154] Organizations could save as much as $402 billion yearly from 2027 to 2040.[150] If the Value of Water Campaign's figures are close to accurate, and if governments around the U.S. acted on them, the necessary $82 billion investment would generate more jobs than the current workforce of 16 states.[150] For every $1 million invested, up to 15 jobs could be generated; six of which would be "direct" jobs in improving the water infrastructure – construction, water conversation managers, urban planners – and nine "indirect" jobs, such as companies that supply the machinery needed for the repairs.[156] Thus, certain industries like construction and water management could flourish, while agricultural industries and other water-dependent sectors may end up paying a lot of money to make the crucial repairs.

One recent approach to water management and water policy that may increase in future is Integrated Water Management (IWM).[154] IWM is a popular term for a strategy that "considers the urban water cycle as a single integrated system."[154] Some cities have already made progress through IWM practices. Los Angeles, for example, plans to increase the volume of stormwater captured from 9 to 50 billion gallons by 2035.[157] This may present opportunities for public–private partnerships, and also a voice to other organizations that hope to be a proactive part of water management, though there will also be challenges. A 2017 study on IWM in India found how difficult IWM can be. By interviewing members of nine government ministries, the researchers found that "lack of capacity, which includes knowledge of climate change and lack of financial resources, technology, and infrastructure were the most cited barrier[s]" to successful IWM.[158] This study highlights one possible area of business that will see increased revenue: Water management analysts and water management educators. As Jacobs and Fleming note: "historical conditions are no longer a reliable basis for future planning" when it comes to water management.[149] Organizations could help nations bogged down in bureaucracy by advocating for both bottom-up and top-down strategies, using their capital and their expertise to influence local policymakers.

In sum, few resources are more important to all organizations than water, since it is a vital resource necessary to support human life. Climate change could continue to create extremes in the water cycle through intense droughts and powerful storms. To ensure that clean drinking water is available to keep a population healthy, locals could continue to develop and adapt water management policies and plans, and perhaps continue to adopt IWM methods to bring together ways of conserving and cleaning water, and this could be in partnership with private organizations.

References

1   Mayer, J. 2010. Covert operations. *New Yorker*, 30 August 2010. https://www.new yorker.com/magazine/2010/08/30/covert-operations, accessed 3 November 2017.

2   Klima, K. and S. Winkelman. 2012. Extreme weather trends, climate science, and public opinion. Center for Clean Air Policy. http://ccap.org/extreme-weather-trend s-climate-science-and-public-opinion/, accessed 27 November 2015.

3   Painter, J. 2011. Poles apart: The international reporting of climate change scepticism. Reuters Institute for the Study of Journalism. http://reutersinstitute.politics.ox.ac.uk/ sites/default/files/research/files/Poles%2520Apart%2520the%2520international%2520rep orting%2520of%2520climate%2520scepticism.pdf, accessed 3 November 2017.

4   Willman, D. 2010. Media and public education, in *Climate Change: Science and Policy*, ed. S. Schneider, et al. Washington, DC: Island Press. pp. 414–420.

5   Kalhoefer, K. 2010. How broadcast networks covered climate change in 2016. *Media Matters*, 23 March 2017. https://www.mediamatters.org/research/2017/03/23/how-broa dcast-networks-covered-climate-change-2016/215718, accessed 5 November 2017.

6   Svoboda, J. 2017. The impact of Brexit on the UK's climate change policy. *Paris Innovation Review*, 5 April 2017. http://parisinnovationreview.com/articles-en/ the-impact-of-brexit-on-the-uks-climate-change-policy, accessed 4 November 2017.

7   Chemnick, J. 2017. Cities and states are picking up Trump's slack on climate, *Scientific American*, 22 September 2017. https://www.scientificamerican.com/article/cities-a nd-states-are-picking-up-trumps-slack-on-climate/.

8   Greshko, M. 2017. Map shows growing U.S. 'climate rebellion' against Trump, *National Geographic*, 8 June 2017. https://news.nationalgeographic.com/2017/06/states-cities-usa -climate-policy-environment/.

9   America's Pledge. 2016. America's Pledge on Climate. https://www.americaspledgeon climate.com, accessed 4 November 2017.

10 Bryan, B. 2017. Trump's pulling the US out of the Paris Climate Agreement could be dis- astrous for the economy. *Business Insider*. https://www.businessinsider.com/trump-lea ving-paris-climate-agreement-effect-on-us-global-economy-2017-6, accessed 5 November 2017.

11 Cook, J., D. Nuccitelli, S.A. Green, M. Richardson, B. Winkler, R. Painting, R. Way, P. Jacobs and A. Skuce. 2013. Quantifying the consensus on anthropogenic global warming in the scientific literature, *Environmental Research Letters*, 8/2: 024024.

12 Liptak, A. 2010. Justices, 5–4, reject corporate spending limit, *New York Times*, 21 January 2010.

13 Andersen, S.S. and K.A. Eliassen. 1995. EU lobbying: The new research agenda, *European Journal of Political Research*, 27/4: 427–441.

14 Drutman, L. 2010. The Business of America is Lobbying: The Expansion of Corporate Political Activity and the Future of American Pluralism, PhD thesis, University of California, Berkeley.

15 Schueth, S. 2003. Socially responsible investing in the United States, *Journal of Business Ethics*, 43/3: 189–194.

16 Wagemans, F.A.J., C.S.A. van Koppen and A.P.J. Mol. 2013. The effectiveness of socially responsible investment: A review, *Journal of Integrative Environmental Sciences*, 10/ 3–4: 235–252.

17 Rehbein, K., J. Logsdon and H. Buren. 2013. Corporate responses to shareholder activists: Considering the dialogue alternative, *Journal of Business Ethics*, 112/1: 137–154.

18 Medland, D. 2017. Europe accounts for over half of $22.89T global SRI assets as sustainable investing takes off, *Forbes*, 27 March 2017.

19 Morgan Stanley. 2017. Sustainable signals: New data from the individual investor. Morgan Stanley Institute for Sustainable Investing. https://www.morganstanley.com/pub/content/dam/msdotcom/ideas/sustainable-signals/pdf/Sustainable_Signals_Whitepaper.pdf, accessed 23 Dec 2017.

20 Drucker, D.J. 2009. From SRI to ESG, *Financial Planning*, 39/10: 72–77.

21 Jeong hwan, P. and N. Jung hee. 2018. Relationship between climate change risk and cost of capital, *Global Business & Finance Review*, 23/2: 66–81.

22 Berridge, R. 2017. Four mutual fund giants begin to address climate change risks in proxy votes: How about your funds? ceres.org, 21 December 2017. https://www.ceres.org/news-center/blog/four-mutual-fund-giants-begin-address-climate-change-risks-proxy-votes-how-about, accessed 22 December 2017.

23 Keitz, A. 2017. Occidental to produce climate risk report in 2018. The Street, 15 December 2017. https://www.thestreet.com/story/14421477/1/occidental-to-produce-climate-risk-report-in-2018.html, accessed 23 December 2017.

24 Fouche, G. 2017. Swedish pension fund sells out of 6 firms it says breach Paris Climate Deal. *Reuters*, 15 June 2017. https://www.reuters.com/article/climatechange-investment-sweden/swedish-pension-fund-sells-out-of-6-firms-it-says-breach-paris-climate-deal-idUSL8N1JC4ME, accessed 23 Dec 2017.

25 Millay, T. 2016. Social investing: The good, the bad, and the ugly, *Forbes*, 29 February 2016.

26 Morgan Stanley Institute for Sustainable Investing. 2015. *Sustainable Reality: Understanding the Performance of Sustainable Investment Strategies*. www.morganstanley.com/sustainableinvesting/pdf/sustainable-reality.pdf, accessed 23 December 2017.

27 Kramer, L. 2017. As millennials age into investors, socially conscious funds boom. *The Observer*, 29 September 2017. observer.com/2017/09/socially-conscious-funds-increase-in-popularity-as-millennials-become-investors/, accessed 23 December 2017.

28 *The Economist*. 2017. Sustainable investment joins the mainstream, 25 November 2017. https://www.economist.com/news/finance-and-economics/21731640-millennials-are-coming-money-and-want-invest-it-responsibly-sustainable, accessed 23 December 2017.

29 Bruckner, T., I.A. Bashmakov, Y. Mulugetta, H. Chum, A. de la Vega Navarro, J. Edmonds, A. Faaij, B. Fungtammasan, A. Garg, E. Hertwich, D. Honnery, D. Infield, M. Kainuma, S. Khennas, S. Kim, H.B. Nimir, K. Riahi, N. Strachan, R. Wiser and X. Zhang. 2014. Energy systems, in *Climate Change 2014: Mitigation of Climate Change. Contribution of Working Group III to the Fifth Assessment Report of the Intergovernmental Panel on Climate Change*, Intergovernmental Panel on Climate Change.

30 IPCC. 2014. *Climate Change 2014: Synthesis Report. Contribution of Working Groups I, II and III to the Fifth Assessment Report of the Intergovernmental Panel on Climate Change*, ed. R.K. Pachauri and L.A. Meyer. Geneva: IPCC.

31 REN21. 2016. *Renewables 2016 Global Status Report Renewable Energy Policy Network for the 21st Century*. http://www.ren21.net/wp-content/uploads/2016/05/GSR_2016_Full_Report_lowres.pdf, accessed 12 July 2017.

32 RE100. 2017. *History of RE100*. RE100. http://there100.org/re100, accessed 12 July 2017.

33 Climate Week NYC. 2015. Going 100% renewable makes basic business sense to IKEA, Infosys and Marks and Spencer. http://www.climateweeknyc.org/news-media/going-100-renewable-makes-basic-business-sense-to-ikea-infosys-and-marks-sp accessed 12 July 2017.

34 Athavale, D. 2015. Infosys is first Indian company to join RE100 global renewal energy campaign, *Times of India*, 18 May 2015.

35 Majmudar, U. and N. Rana. 2016. Infosys to source 100% power from renewables by 2018: Ramadas Kamath, *The Economic Times*. http://economictimes.indiatimes.com/op

inion/interviews/infosys-to-source-100-power-from-renewables-by-2018-ramadas-kamath
/articleshow/53871502.cms, accessed 8 October 2018.

36 Peters, A. 2017. Electric Truck Company Chanje has a plan to clean up urban freight. *Fast
    Company*. https://www.fastcompany.com/40451737/electric-truck-company-chanje-has
    -a-plan-to-clean-up-urban-freight?utm_source=Clean+Energy+Review&utm_campa
    ign=9d7c0ac205-EMAIL_CAMPAIGN_2017_08_14-CER&utm_medium=email&utm_
    term=0_08b98425f1-9d7c0ac205-341834105, accessed 5 August 2018.

37 Interface. 2017. Interface unveils prototype carpet tile to inspire new approaches to address
    climate change. Interface. http://www.interface.com/US/en-US/about/press-room/ca
    rbon-storing-tile-release-en_US, accessed 5 August 2018.

38 International Energy Agency. 2015. *India Energy Outlook: A World Energy Outlook
    Special Report*, International Energy Agency.

39 Giannakopoulou, E. and S. Henbest. 2016. New energy outlook 2016. *Bloomberg New
    Energy Finance*. https://www.bnef.com/dataview/new-energy-outlook-2016/index.
    html#section-0, accessed 5 August 2018.

40 Berke, J. 2017. One type of energy is killing fossil fuels. *Business Insider*. http://www.
    businessinsider.com/renewable-energy-is-killing-fossil-fuels-2016-4?r=US&IR=T&
    IR=T, accessed 12 July 2017.

41 Landberg, R. 2017. Clean electricity revolution poised to steamroll fossil fuels as cost
    of renewables plunges. *Independent*. https://www.independent.co.uk/news/science/
    clean-electricity-revolution-fossil-fuels-renewable-costs-plunge-green-technology-a
    7956826.html, accessed 5 August 2018.

42 Samuelson, K. 2017. Renewable energy is creating jobs 12 times faster than the rest of the
    economy. *Fortune*. http://fortune.com/2017/01/27/solar-wind-renewable-jobs/, accessed
    12 July 2017.

43 United Nations World Water Assessment Programme and UN-Water. 2018. *The
    United Nations World Water Development Report 2018: Nature-Based Solutions for Water*.
    Paris: UNESCO.

44 U.S. Department of Energy. 2018. Water-efficient technology opportunities. U.S.
    Department of Energy Office of Energy Efficiency and Renewable Energy. https://www.
    energy.gov/eere/femp/water-efficient-technology-opportunities, accessed 26 August 2018.

45 Sovocool, K., M. Morgan and M. Drinkwine. 2009. *Field Study of Uniformity Improvements
    from Multi-Stream Rotational Spray Heads and Associated Products*. Southern Nevada Water
    Authority, 21 October 2009. http://www.irrigation.org/IA/FileUploads/IA/Resources/
    TechnicalPapers/2009/FieldStudyOfUniformityImprovementsFromMulti-StreamRota
    tionalSprayHeadsAndAssociatedProducts-PreliminaryResults.pdf, accessed 26 August 2018.

46 Kulkarni, S. 2011. Innovative technologies for water saving in irrigated agriculture,
    International Journal of Water Resources and Arid Environments, 1/3: 226–231.

47 Koel, J. 2013. How 5 manufacturers reduce water use. Fabricators & Manufacturers
    Association International, 27 July 2013. https://www.fmanet.org/blog/2013/07/27/
    5-manufacturers-reduce-water-use, accessed 26 August 2018.

48 Gunderson, J. 2013. China's Jinhai pulp facility: Innovation in water conservation and dis-
    charge. *Industrial Water World*, 1 February 2013. https://www.waterworld.com/articles/
    iww/print/volume-13/issue-1/feature-editorial/chinas-jinhai-pulp-facility-innovatio
    n-in-water-conservation-and.html, accessed 26 August 2018.

49 Burek, P., S. Mubareka, R. Rojas, A. De Roo, A. Bianchi, C. Baranzelli, C. Lavalle and I.
    Vandecasteele. 2012. *Evaluation of the Effectiveness of Natural Water Retention Measures: Sup-
    port to the EU Blueprint to Safeguard Europe's Waters*. European Commission/Joint Research
    Centre/Institute for Environment and Sustainability. ec.europa.eu/environment/water/
    blueprint/pdf/EUR25551EN_JRC_Blueprint_NWRM.pdf accessed 26 August 2018.

50 Dubois, O. 2011. *The State of the World's Land and Water Resources for Food and Agriculture: Managing Systems at Risk.* Abingdon, UK and New York: Earthscan.

51 Marchal, V., R. Dellink, D. van Vuuren, C. Clapp, J. Château, E. Lanzi, B. Magné and J. van Vliet. 2012. *OECD Environmental Outlook to 2050: The Consequences of Inaction.* OECD Publishing: doi:10.1787/9789264122246-en, accessed 26 August 2018.

52 DNV GL, UN Global Compact and Sustainia. 2017. *Global Opportunity Report 2017.* www.globalopportunitynetwork.org/the-2017-global-opportunity-report.pdf, accessed 26 August 2018.

53 Apse, C. and Benjamin Bryant. 2015. *Upper Tana-Nairobi Water Fund: A Business Case.* The Nature Conservancy. https://www.nature.org/ourinitiatives/regions/africa/upper-tana-na irobi-water-fund-business-case.pdf?redirect=https-301, accessed 26 August 2018.

54 Schaible, G.D. and M.P. Aillery. 2012. Water conservation in irrigated agriculture: Trends and challenges in the face of emerging demands, *Economic Information Bulletin,* 99.

55 Business for Social Responsibility. June 2017. *The State of Sustainable Business 2017: Results of the 9th Annual Survey of Sustainable Business Leaders.* Business for Social Responsibility. https://www.bsr.org/files/event-resources/2017_BSR_Webinar_Deck_June26_Final_USE MEA.pdf, accessed 6 December 2017.

56 The Climate Group. 2008. *Consumers, Brands and Climate Change: Helping Businesses to Focus.* The Climate Group. https://www.theclimategroup.org/sites/default/files/archive/files/Consumers_Brands_and_Climate_Change_2008.pdf, accessed 6 December 2017.

57 Bowman, J. April 2008. Climate change: Green branding – Cashing in on the eco-market. *World Intellectual Property Organization Magazine.* http://www.wipo.int/wip o_magazine/en/2008/02/article_0003.html, accessed 6 December 2017.

58 Delmas, M.A. and S. Pekovic. 2013. Environmental standards and labor productivity: Understanding the mechanisms that sustain sustainability, *Journal of Organizational Behavior,* 34: 230–252.

59 Milman, O. 2017. Exxon, BP and Shell back carbon tax proposal to curb emissions. *The Guardian,* 20 June 2017. https://www.theguardian.com/environment/2017/jun/20/exxon-bp-shell-oil-climate-change, accessed 7 December 2017.

60 *The Guardian.* 15 February 2011. Being energy efficient is key to being competitive. *The Guardian.* https://www.theguardian.com/sustainable-business/british-gas-energy-effi ciency-competitive-advantage, accessed 7 December 2017.

61 Whelan, T. and C. Fink. 2016. The comprehensive case for sustainability. *Harvard Business Review.* https://hbr.org/2016/10/the-comprehensive-business-case-for-sustaina bility, accessed 6 December 2017.

62 Sachs, J. 2014. The ultimate missed social-media opportunity for brands: Climate change. *The Guardian,* 12 March 2014. https://www.theguardian.com/sustainable-business/social-marke ting-brands-coke-chevrolet-climate-change-environment, accessed 6 December 2017.

63 Hersch, J. and W.K. Viscusi. 2006. The generational divide in support for environmental policies: European evidence, *Climatic Change,* 77/1–2: 121–136.

64 Nuccitelli, D. 2016. The climate change generation gap. *Bulletin of Atomic Scientists,* 21 April 2016. https://thebulletin.org/climate-change-generation-gap9351, accessed 6 December 2017.

65 Lewis, P. and J. Woods. 2014. The generation gap on climate change. *ABC News.* http://www.abc.net.au/news/2014-04-08/lewis-and-woods-the-generation-gap-on-clima te-change/5374618, accessed 6 December 2017.

66 Goffee, R. and G. Jones. 2013. Creating the best workplace on earth, *Harvard Business Review,* 91/5: 98–106.

67 Practical Law Company. 2018. Public private partnerships: Issues and considerations. American Bar Association. http://apps.americanbar.org/dch/thedl.cfm?filename=/CL113000/site

sofinterest_files/PublicPrivatePartnershipsIssuesandConsiderations.pdf, accessed 24 February 2018.

68 Koh, D. 2017. An overview of public-private partnerships. *OpenGov Asia*, 29 November 2017. https://www.opengovasia.com/articles/7361-an-overview-of-public-private-partnerships, accessed 28 February 2018.

69 Bhagat, V. and A. Skromme. 2011. Natural allies: The government and the private sector need each other to advance the climate agenda, *Handshake*, 2 July 2011, 6–9.

70 Grant, H. 2016. Five ways public-private partnerships can build healthier cities. *The Guardian*, 19 December 2016. https://www.theguardian.com/global-development-professionals-network/2016/dec/19/five-ways-public-private-partnerships-can-build-healthier-cities, accessed 28 February 2018.

71 C40 Cities. 2015. Cities100: Washington, D.C. – Wind Power Purchase Saves Money. C40 Cities, 30 October 2015. http://www.c40.org/case_studies/cities100-washington-d-c-wind-power-purchase-saves-money accessed 28 February 2018.

72 The City of New York. 2014. *Mayor's Office of Long-Term Planning and Sustainability, One City: Built to Last*. The City of New York. http://www.nyc.gov/html/builttolast/assets/downloads/pdf/OneCity.pdf, accessed 28 February 2018.

73 Hindustan Construction Company. 2015. *Responsible Infrastructure: Sustainability Report 2014–2015*. Hindustan Construction Company: http://www.hccindia.com/csr_bread/Sustainability_report_2014-15.pdf, accessed 28 February 2018.

74 Desai, V. 2012. HCC only Indian company to be featured [sic] climate report by UNEP. *Economic Times*, 18 June 2012. https://economictimes.indiatimes.com/news/company/corporate-trends/hcc-only-indian-company-to-be-featured-climate-report-by-unep/articleshow/14243316.cms, accessed 28 February 2018.

75 UN Global Compact and Environment Programme. 2012. *Business and Climate Change Adaptation: Toward Resilient Companies and Communities*. Caring for Climate. caringforclimate.org/wp-content/uploads/Business_and_Climate_Change_Adaptation.pdf, accessed 28 February 2018.

76 India Resource Center. 2016. Disputed Coca-Cola plant shut down in India: Deteriorated groundwater conditions lead to closure. India Resource Center, 10 February 2016. http://www.indiaresource.org/news/2016/1003.html, accessed 28 February 2018.

77 Perard, E. 2011. Renewable energy trends: Low- & middle-income countries, *Handshake*, 2 July: 16–18.

78 Agard, J. and L. Schipper. 2014. WGII AR5 glossary, in *Climate Change 2014: Impacts, Adaptation, and Vulnerability. Contribution of Working Group II to the Fifth Assessment Report of the Intergovernmental Panel on Climate Change*, ed. J. Birkmann, et al. Cambridge and New York: Cambridge University Press. pp. 1439–1498.

79 Elkins, K. 2015. 22-year sea level rise – TOPEX/JASON. NASA. https://svs.gsfc.nasa.gov/cgi-bin/details.cgi?aid=4345, accessed 4 May 2017.

80 Tompkins, F. and C. Deconcini. 2014. *Sea-level rise and its impact on Miami-Dade County*. World Resources Institute. http://www.wri.org/sites/default/files/sealevelrise_miami_florida_factsheet_final.pdf, accessed 1 August 2017.

81 Miami-Dade County. *Miami-Dade County Climate Action Plan*. Miami-Dade County. http://www.miamidade.gov/greenprint/pdf/climate_action_plan.pdf, accessed 4 May 2017.

82 Union of Concerned Scientists. 2017. When rising seas hit home: An analysis by the Union of Concerned Scientists. Union of Concerned Scientists. https://ucsusa.maps.arcgis.com/apps/MapSeries/index.html?appid=64b2cbd03a3d4b87aaddaf65f6b33332&entry=2, accessed 5 July 2017.

83 Kallergis, K. 2016. Which Miami condo towers will be most affected by sea level rise? *The Real Deal: South Florida Real Estate News*. https://therealdeal.com/miami/2016/02/

29/which-miami-condo-towers-will-be-most-affected-by-sea-level-rise-map/, accessed 14 August 2017.

84 Ruggeri, A. 2017. Miami's fight against rising seas. *BBC*. http://www.bbc.com/future/story/20170403-miamis-fight-against-sea-level-rise, accessed 15 August 2017.

85 Moulite, J. 2017. Color of climate: Meet a power player in Miami's fight against climate gentrification. *The Root*. http://www.theroot.com/color-of-climate-meet-a-power-player-in-miami-s-fight-1797702979?utm_medium=sharefromsite&utm_source=The_Root_twitter, accessed 13 August 2017.

86 Arraf, J. 2017. In Egypt, a rising sea – and growing worries about climate change's effects. *NPR*: http://www.npr.org/sections/parallels/2017/08/13/542645647/in-egypt-a-rising-sea-and-growing-worries-about-climate-changes-effects, accessed 14 August 2017.

87 PG&E Corporation. 2017. *Annual Report Pursuant to Section 13 of or 15(d) of the Securities Exchange Act of 1934 for the Fiscal Year Ended December 31, 2016*. Securities and Exchange Commission. https://www.sec.gov/Archives/edgar/data/1004980/000100498017000006/form10k.htm, accessed 4 May 2017.

88 Cole, S. 2015. NASA Science Zeros in on Ocean Rise: How Much? How Soon? National Aeronautics and Space Administration. https://www.nasa.gov/press-release/nasa-science-zeros-in-on-ocean-rise-how-much-how-soon, accessed 4 May 2017.

89 Hansen, J., M. Sato, P. Hearty, R. Ruedy, M. Kelley, V. Masson-Delmotte, G. Russell, G. Tselioudis, J. Cao, E. Rignot, I. Velicogna, B. Tormey, B. Donovan, E. Kandiano, K. von Schuckmann, P. Kharecha, A.N. Legrande, M. Bauer and K.W. Lo. 2016. Ice melt, sea level rise and superstorms: Evidence from paleoclimate data, climate modeling, and modern observations that 2°C global warming could be dangerous, *Atmospheric Chemistry and Physics*, 16/6: 3761–3812.

90 IPCC. 2018. *Global Warming of 1.5°C*. Intergovernmental Panel on Climate Change. http://ipcc.ch/report/sr15/, accessed 13 October 2018.

91 Bojnansky, E. 2016. Miami Beach property values may fall as sea levels rise: Experts. *The Real Deal: South Florida Real Estate News*. https://therealdeal.com/miami/2016/04/07/miami-beach-property-values-may-fall-as-sea-levels-rise-experts/, accessed 25 July 2017.

92 Kallergis, K. 2016. Miami faces $3.5T loss, highest risk of sea level rise among all coastal cities: Report. *The Real Deal: South Florida Real Estate News*. https://therealdeal.com/miami/2016/08/16/miami-faces-3-5t-loss-highest-risk-of-sea-level-rise-among-all-coastal-cities-report/, accessed 14 August 2017.

93 Hinkel, J., D. Lincke, A.T. Vafeidis, M. Perrette, R.J. Nicholls, R.S. Tol, B. Marzeion, X. Fettweis, C. Ionescu and A. Levermann. 2014. Coastal flood damage and adaptation costs under 21st century sea-level rise, *Proceedings of the National Academy of Sciences*, 111/9: 3292–3297.

94 IPCC. 2014. *Climate Change 2014: Impacts, Adaptation, and Vulnerability. Part B: Regional Aspects. Contribution of Working Group II to the Fifth Assessment Report of the Intergovernmental Panel on Climate Change*, ed. V.R. Barros, et al. Cambridge & New York: Cambridge University Press.

95 Thomson Reuters Foundation. 2017. Australia heat wave causes firms to power down but blackouts avoided. *Thomson Reuters Foundation News*. http://news.trust.org/item/20170210050229-deq66/, accessed 21 May 2017.

96 Sivakumar, M.V.K. and R. Stefanski. 2010. Chapter 2: Climate change in South Asia, in *Climate Change and Food Security in South Asia*, ed. R. Lal, et al. The Netherlands: Springer.

97 UNBC. 2018. *Climate Change and the Mountain Pine Beetle*. University of Northern British Columbia. https://www.unbc.ca/releases/2007/climate-change-and-mountain-pine-beetle, accessed 4 August 2018.

98   Haile, M.G., W. Tesfamicheal, T. Kindie and J. von Braun. 2017. Impact of climate change, weather extremes, and price risk on global food supply, *Economics of Disasters and Climate Change*, 1/1: 55–75.

99   NOAA. 2018. How does climate change affect coral reefs? National Ocean Service. https://oceanservice.noaa.gov/facts/coralreef-climate.html, accessed 3 August 2018.

100 Fishman, A. 2018. *Without Climate Action, UNESCO Projects Disappearance of Coral Reefs by 2100*. International Institute for Sustainable Development. http://sdg.iisd.org/news/without-climate-action-unesco-projects-disappearance-of-coral-reefs-by-2100/, accessed 3 August 2018.

101 Halper, E. 2018. Racing to save Florida's coral from climate change, scientists turn to a once-unthinkable strategy: 'assisted evolution'. *Los Angeles Times*. http://www.latimes.com/science/sciencenow/la-na-pol-coral-climate-change-20180709-htmlstory.html, accessed 3 August 2018.

102 Bureau of Meteorology. 2018. *Climate Glossary*. Australian Government Bureau of Meteorology. http://www.bom.gov.au/climate/glossary/precipitation.shtml, accessed 4 August 2018.

103 Union of Concerned Scientists. 2013. *Overwhelming Risk: Rethinking Flood Insurance in a World of Rising Seas*. http://www.ucsusa.org/global_warming/science_and_impacts/impacts/flood-insurance-sea-level-rise.html, accessed 2 June 2017.

104 U.S. Global Change Research Program. 2014. *Extreme Weather*. http://nca2014.globalchange.gov/highlights/report-findings/extreme-weather, accessed 8 June 2017.

105 ClimateWise. 2016. *Investing for Resilience*. https://www.cisl.cam.ac.uk/publications/publication-pdfs/Investing-for-resilience.pdf, accessed 7 June 2017.

106 National Association of Insurance Commissioners. 2017. *Climate Risk Disclosure Survey*. http://www.insurance.ca.gov/0250-insurers/0300-insurers/0100-applications/ClimateSurvey/, accessed 9 June 2017.

107 van Vliet, M.T.H., D. Wiberg, S. Leduc and K. Riahi. 2016. Power-generation system vulnerability and adaptation to changes in climate and water resources, *Nature Climate Change*, 6/4: 375–380.

108 Satran, J. 2015. 2 simple maps that reveal how American agriculture actually works. *Huffington Post*. https://www.huffingtonpost.com/2015/01/16/largest-crop-each-state_n_6488930.html, accessed 4 August 2018.

109 U.S. Global Change Research Program. 2014. *Extreme Weather*. U.S. Global Change Research Program. http://nca2014.globalchange.gov/highlights/report-findings/extreme-weather, accessed 8 October 2018.

110 Estrada, F., W.W. Botzen and R.S. Tol. 2015. Economic losses from US hurricanes consistent with an influence from climate change, *Nature Geoscience*, 8/11: 880.

111 Knabb, R.D., J.R. Rhome and D.P. Brown. 2005. *Tropical Cyclone Report: Hurricane Katrina, 23–30 August 2005*. National Hurricane Center, 20 December 2005. http://www.nhc.noaa.gov/data/tcr/AL122005_Katrina.pdf, accessed 8 October 2018.

112 Garamone, J. 2015. Remembering Hurricane Katrina a decade later. U.S. Department of Defense, 28 August 2015. https://www.defense.gov/News/Article/Article/615149/remembering-hurricane-katrina-a-decade-later/, accessed 15 June 2017.

113 Rushton, C. 2015. Timeline: Hurricane Katrina and the aftermath. *USA Today*, 24 August 2015. https://www.usatoday.com/story/news/nation/2015/08/24/timeline-hurricane-katrina-and-aftermath/32003013/, accessed 15 June 2017.

114 National Hurricane Center. 2018. Costliest U.S. tropical cyclones tables updated. National Oceanic and Atmospheric Administration, 26 January 2018. https://www.nhc.noaa.gov/news/UpdatedCostliest.pdf, accessed 8 October 2018.

115 Barlyn, S. 2017. Business interrupted: hurricane-damaged firms dig in for insurance fight. Reuters, 15 September 2017. https://www.reuters.com/article/us-storm-irma -insurance-businesses/business-interrupted-hurricane-damaged-firms-dig-in-for-insura nce-fight-idUSKCN1BQ0EY?utm_source=applenews, accessed 8 October 2018.

116 Lubber, M. 28 September 2017. Following hurricane devastation, calls to bring back the Federal Flood Standards get louder. Forbes, 28 September 2017. https://www.forbes.com/ sites/mindylubber/2017/09/28/following-hurricane-devastation-calls-to-bring-back-the-federal-flood-standards-get-louder/#3215219c3694, accessed 8 October 2018.

117 Abrams, R. 2017. How climate change can hit your small business. USA Today, 13 September 2017. https://www.usatoday.com/story/money/columnist/abrams/2017/09/13/how-climate-change-can-hit-your-small-business/623345001/, accessed 8 October 2018.

118 United Nations Framework Convention on Climate Change. UNFCCC website. http:// unfccc.int/, accessed 21 July 2017.

119 UNFCCC. The Paris Agreement. United Nations Framework Convention on Climate Change. https://unfccc.int/process/the-paris-agreement/what-is-the-paris-agreement, accessed 13 October 2018.

120 World Nuclear Association. June2017. Policy Responses to Climate Change. http:// www.world-nuclear.org/information-library/energy-and-the-environment/policy-r esponses-to-climate-change.aspx, accessed 29 August 2017.

121 Ministry of Environment Forest and Climate Change. National Action Plan on Climate Change. Government of India. http://www.moef.nic.in/ccd-napcc, accessed 7 September 2017.

122 Government of India. 2015. India surging ahead in the field of Green Energy – 100 GW Solar Scale-Up plan. http://pib.nic.in/newsite/PrintRelease.aspx?relid=122566, accessed 7 September 2017.

123 Kumar, V.R. 2017. India adds 4.8 GW of solar capacity in H1. The Hindu Business Line. http://www.thehindubusinessline.com/news/india-adds-48-gw-of-solar-capacity-in-h1/ article9808471.ece, accessed 7 September 2017.

124 Galston, W.A., S. Gross, M. Muro, T. Roberts, R. Tongia, D.G. Victor, P.A. Wallach, R. Winthrop, C. Kwauk, N. Hultman, T. Stern and V. Thomas. 2017. Trump's Paris Agreement withdrawal: What it means and what comes next. Brookings, accessed 2 September 2017.

125 The White House. 2016. United States Mid-Century Strategy for deep decarbonisation. The White House. https://unfccc.int/files/focus/long-term_strategies/applica tion/pdf/mid_century_strategy_report-final_red.pdf, accessed 1 September 2017.

126 BBC. 2017. Paris climate deal: Dismay as Trump signals exit from accord. http://www. bbc.com/news/world-us-canada-40128431, accessed 31 August 2017.

127 The White House. 2013. The President's Climate Action Plan. https://obamawhitehouse. archives.gov/sites/default/files/image/president27sclimateactionplan.pdf, accessed 4 September 2017.

128 Stern, N. 2006. The Economics of Climate Change: The Stern Review. Cambridge: Cambridge University Press.

129 Elgie, S., R. Beaty and R. Lipsey. 2014. British Columbia's Carbon Tax Shift: An Environmental and Economic Success. World Bank. http://blogs.worldbank.org/climatechange/ british-columbia-s-carbon-tax-shift-environmental-and-economic-success, accessed 10 September 2017.

130 P.F. 2014. The evidence mounts. The Economist. https://www.economist.com/blogs/am ericasview/2014/07/british-columbias-carbon-tax, accessed 10 September 2017.

131 Global Commission on the Economy and Climate. 2014. Better Growth, Better Climate: The Synthesis Report. The New Climate Economy, World Resources Institute. http://static.

newclimateeconomy.report/wp-content/uploads/2014/08/NCE_SynthesisReport.pdf, accessed 18 September 2018.

132 Rivers, N. and B. Schaufele. 2014. The effect of British Columbia's carbon tax on agricultural trade. Pacific Institute for Climate Solutions. http://pics.uvic.ca/sites/default/files/uploads/publications/Carbon%20Tax%20on%20Agricultural%20Trade_0.pdf, accessed 10 September 2017.

133 Nauclér, T. and P.-A. Enkvist. 2009. Pathways to a low-carbon economy: Version 2 of the global greenhouse gas abatement cost curve, McKinsey & Company.

134 Haigh, N. 2008. A view backstage of climate change environmental markets, *Australasian Journal of Environmental Management*, 15: 76–83.

135 Enkvist, P.-A., T. Nauclér and J.M. Oppenheim. 2008. Business strategies for climate change, *The McKinsey Quarterly*, 2: 24–33.

136 van Ee, B. 2015. Businesses can benefit from climate targets, but only if they adapt. Euractiv. https://www.euractiv.com/section/innovation-industry/opinion/businesses-can-benefit-from-climate-targets-but-only-if-they-adapt/, accessed 29 August 2017.

137 Crooks, E. 2017. Trump climate policy risks more jobs than it saves. *Financial Times*. https://www.ft.com/content/6a5fa710-46ea-11e7-8d27-59b4dd6296b8, accessed 29 August 2017.

138 Bioenergy International AG. 2016. *Production Statistics*. Bioenergy International A.: http://biodiesel.org/production/production-statistics, accessed 7 September 2017.

139 Renewable Fuels Association. 2012. Jobs, economic opportunity, energy security define ethanol. *Ethanol Producer Magazine*. http://ethanolproducer.com/articles/8596/jobs-economic-opportunity-energy-security-define-ethanol, accessed 7 September 2017.

140 Kerr, T., A. Maheshwari and J. Sottong. 2016. *Climate Investment Opportunities in Emerging Markets: An IFC Analysis*. International Finance Corporation. http://www.ifc.org/wps/wcm/connect/51183b2d-c82e-443e-bb9b-68d9572dd48d/3503-IFC-Climate_Investment_Opportunity-Report-Dec-FINAL.pdf?MOD=AJPERES, accessed 4 September 2017.

141 López-Gómez, C., S.M. Gregory and E. O'Sullivan. 2013. *Emerging Trends in Global Manufacturing Industries*. United Nations Industrial Development Organization. https://www.unido.org/fileadmin/user_media/Services/PSD/Emerging_Trends_UNIDO_2013.PDF, accessed 4 September 2017.

142 Goldman Sachs. 2015. *The Low Carbon Economy*. Goldman Sachs. http://www.goldmansachs.com/our-thinking/pages/new-energy-landscape-folder/report-the-low-carbon-economy/report.pdf, accessed 3 September 2017.

143 O'Sullivan, D.F. and C.H. Warren. 2016. *Solar Securitization: An Innovation in Renewable Energy*. MIT Energy Initiative: https://energy.mit.edu/wp-content/uploads/2016/07/MITEI-WP-2016-05.pdf, accessed 11 September 2017.

144 United Nations Environmental Program. 2016. *The Adaptation Gap Report*. United Nations Environmental Program. http://drustage.unep.org/adaptationgapreport/sites/unep.org.adaptationgapreport/files/documents/agr2016.pdf, accessed 10 September 2017.

145 Stern, N. and D. Zenghelis. 2015. Climate change and cities: A prime source of problems, yet key to a solution, *The Guardian*, 19 November 2015: https://www.theguardian.com/cities/2015/nov/17/cities-climate-change-problems-solution, accessed 10 September 2017.

146 World Bank. 2015. 5 ways to reduce the drivers of climate change. World Bank, 18 March 2015. http://www.worldbank.org/en/news/feature/2015/03/18/5-ways-reduce-drivers-climate-change, accessed 10 September 2017.

147 Beinhocker, E. and J. Oppenheim. 2014. Economic opportunities in a low-carbon world. UNFCCC. http://unfccc.int/press/news_room/newsletter/guest_column/items/4608.php, accessed 2 September 2017.

148 Newton, J. 2015. The 'water wars' trap. *Slate*, 9 December 2015. www.slate.com/arti cles/technology/future_tense/2015/12/water_wars_caused_by_climate_change_aren_t_ something_we_need_to_worry_about.html, accessed 4 February 2018.

149 Jacobs, K. and P. Fleming. 2017. Climate change: A strategic opportunity for water managers, in *The Water Problem: Climate Change and Water Policy in the United States*, ed. P. Mulroy. Washington D.C.: Brookings.

150 Quinn, A., K. Feeney and H. Castro. 2017. The economic benefits of investing in water infrastructure. Value of Water Campaign. http://thevalueofwater.org/sites/defa ult/files/Economic%20Impact%20of%20Investing%20in%20Water%20Infrastructure_ VOW_FINAL_pages.pdf, accessed 4 February 2018.

151 DeFlorio-Barker, S., C. Wing, R.M. Jones and S. Dorevitch. 2018. Estimate of inci- dence and cost of recreational waterborne illness on United States surface waters, *Environmental Health*, 17/1: 3.

152 National Center for Environmental Assessment. *Estimating the Burden of Disease Asso- ciated with Outbreaks Reported to the U.S. Waterborne Disease Outbreak Surveillance System: Identifying Limitations and Improvements*. U.S. Environmental Protection Agency. https:// ofmpub.epa.gov/eims/eimscomm.getfile?p_download_id=470886, accessed 4 February 2018.

153 Chen, M. 2018. Trump's infrastructure plan could destroy our nation's water systems. *The Nation*, 30 January 2018. https://www.thenation.com/article/trumps-infrastruc ture-plan-could-destroy-our-nations-water-systems/, accessed 4 February 2018.

154 Meder, M. and S. Rhodes-Conway. June 2016. *Integrated Water Management: A Guide for City Leader 2016*. Mayors Innovation Project. https://www.mayorsinnovation.org/ images/uploads/pdf/Water_brief.pdf, accessed 4 February 2018.

155 American Water Works Association. 2012. *Buried No Longer: Confronting America's Water Infrastructure Challenge*. American Water Works Association: https://www.awwa. org/Portals/0/files/legreg/documents/BuriedNoLonger.pdf, accessed 4 February 2018.

156 Crow, P. New report highlights staggering costs ahead for water infrastructure. *Water- world*. http://www.waterworld.com/articles/print/volume-28/issue-4/departments/wa shington-update/new-report-highlights-staggering-costs-ahead-for-water-infrastruc ture-by-patrick-crow-washington-correspondent.html, accessed 4 February 2018.

157 Black, H. 2017. Alabama faces another drought season with no plan for water use; Gov- ernor shifts direction in who will produce one. *Birmingham Watch*, 30 November 2017. https://birminghamwatch.org/alabama-faces-another-drought-season-no-plan-water- use-governor-shifts-direction-will-produce-one/, accessed 5 February 2018.

158 Azhoni, A., I. Holman and S. Jude. 2017. Adapting water management to climate change: Institutional involvement, inter-institutional networks and barriers in India, *Global Environmental Change*, 44: 144–149.

INDEX

Page numbers in **bold** refer to figures, page numbers in *italic* refer to tables.

CPSIA information can be obtained
at www.ICGtesting.com
Printed in the USA
LVHW011953151221
706295LV00004B/195